"We hold these truths to be self-evident, that all men are created equal, that they are endowed by their Creator with certain unalienable Rights, that among these are Life, Liberty and the pursuit of Happiness."

— Declaration of Independence

Historic PHILADELPHIA

★ OFFICIAL GUIDEBOOK ★

BECKON BOOKS

INDEPENDENCE VISITOR CENTER CORPORATION

SEAL OF THE CITY OF PHILADELPHIA

gp tmc
Greater Philadelphia Tourism Marketing Corp
visitphilly.com

PHLCVB
Philadelphia Convention & Visitors Bureau

PA

CONTENTS

Planning Your Visit

Welcome to Philadelphia, birthplace of the United States of America. Established in 1682 by William Penn, Philadelphia played a central role in the founding of our nation. Philadelphia was the site where the Declaration of Independence and the Constitution of the United States were both debated and signed. It was also the nation's capital for ten years while Washington, D.C., was being built, and it was home to many 18th century leaders, such as Benjamin Franklin, the writer, printer, ambassador, inventor, scientist, civic leader, and signer of the Declaration of Independence and the U.S. Constitution. Today, Philadelphia has much to offer, including well-preserved 18th, 19th, and 20th century buildings, four units of the National Park System, world-renowned museums and institutions, and shopping, restaurants, and nightlife.

Liberty Bell: The Liberty Bell has drawn people to Philadelphia for more than 150 years. In this 19th century image, the bell hangs from 13 links that represent the 13 original colonies.

Independence Visitor Center: Opened in 2001, the Independence Visitor Center serves as the gateway to Independence National Historical Park. The center sits on the west side of Independence Mall just north of the Liberty Bell Center and Independence Hall.

This official guidebook from the Independence Visitor Center Corporation is designed to help you make the most of your trip to historic Philadelphia. The book contains important tips; sample itineraries; a map of the city, historic district, and national historical park; compelling history about the city, its sites, and people; and a listing of websites in the back. We hope that while visiting Philadelphia, you'll experience its rich culture and learn more about its crucial role in the founding and growth of the United States.

About Philadelphia:
Philadelphia is the second largest city on the East Coast and is home to 1.5 million people. City Hall stands 548 feet tall and is the nation's largest municipal building.

On February 22, 1861, Abraham Lincoln stopped in Philadelphia on his way to Washington, D.C., to take the presidential oath of office. He made a point to visit Independence Hall, where the Declaration of Independence and the U. S. Constitution had been written and signed nearly 100 years earlier.

Independence Hall: The south side of Independence Hall facing Independence Square is the most often photographed part of the building. However, the north side served as the main entrance when the Hall was first built.

During Lincoln's speech to the crowd gathered there, he alluded to the challenges the nation faced—both in 1776 and in 1861. "I am filled with deep emotion at finding myself standing here in the place where were collected together the wisdom, the patriotism, the devotion to principle, from which sprang the institutions under which we live," he said. "I have often pondered over the dangers which were incurred by the men who assembled here, and framed and adopted that Declaration of Independence. . . . It was . . . that sentiment in the Declaration of Independence which gave liberty, not alone to the people of this country, but, I hope, to the world, for all future time."

Carpenters' Hall: Carpenters' Hall witnessed the gathering of delegates for the First Continental Congress in 1774.

Liberty Bell: The Liberty Bell was likely rung on July 8, 1776, to gather Philadelphians to hear the first public reading of the Declaration of Independence.

Since Lincoln's visit, millions of people have come to Philadelphia to experience its rich history and vibrant culture. Like Lincoln, they have been stirred by the words and actions of those Americans who struggled to create an independent nation. Today, with iconic sites like Independence Hall, the Liberty Bell, and Franklin Court in Independence National Historical Park, and the Betsy Ross House, Elfreth's Alley, and Christ Church in the historic district, this cosmopolitan city tells the story of their unwavering strength.

The Independence Visitor Center: The Visitor Center offers event, touring, and lodging information about Greater Philadelphia as well as historical films, refreshments, ticket sales, maps, and brochures.

Philadelphia is the fifth largest city in the United States. Located in the middle of the Northeast Corridor, it is 70 miles south of New York, 100 miles north of Washington, D.C., and within a day's drive of 40 percent of the U.S. population.

Independence National Historical Park: When Congress created the park in 1948, it sparked a successful renewal of the residential neighborhood and urban center around the park.

Whether this is your first time visiting this bustling and historic city or you have been to Philadelphia many times, start your trip at the Independence Visitor Center. Located at 6th and Market streets, across from the Liberty Bell, the Independence Visitor Center is owned by the National Park Service. These two entities jointly staff the building managed by the Independence Visitor Center Corporation. The Visitor Center is the official welcome center of Independence National Historical Park and the Greater Philadelphia Region. It is the exclusive location to pick up free timed tickets to tour Independence Hall. The Visitor Center provides many visitor services, including knowledgeable National Park Service Rangers, a multilingual concierge staff, and on-site ticketing to over 60 area attractions. It offers tours, maps, brochures, daily event listings, free historical films, free wireless Internet access, a snack bar, gift shop, and restrooms.

The Independence Visitor Center is the primary point of orientation for Independence National Historical Park, the City of Philadelphia, and the southern New Jersey and Delaware Waterfronts, as well as Bucks, Chester, Delaware, and Montgomery counties in Pennsylvania.

The Independence Visitor Center Corporation is a nonprofit organization that operates the Independence Visitor Center in cooperation with the National Park Service. The Independence Visitor Center Corporation also supports the efforts of the Greater Philadelphia Tourism Marketing Corporation, the Philadelphia Convention and Visitors Bureau, the City of Philadelphia, and the Commonwealth of Pennsylvania.

1 N. Independence Mall West, Philadelphia, PA 19106 • (800) 537-7676

GETTING AROUND

The simple grid pattern of the streets that William Penn designed back in the 1680s makes the heart of Philadelphia easy to navigate. Main streets running east and west are named after trees (south of Market Street), and streets running north and south are numbered.

The city has an extensive, easy-to-navigate transit system that includes buses, subways, trains, and trolleys. The SEPTA (Southeastern Pennsylvania Transportation Authority) public transportation system offers various packages for families and individuals that provide savings on transit. For more information, contact www.septa.org/welcome or call (215) 580-7800.

District Signage: Philadelphia is a compact and walkable city, with colorful signs placed for pedestrians. There are numerous walking tours, including architectural, historical, ghost, and art and culture tours.

Many of the city's attractions are readily accessible by foot. Color-coded signs for each district will point you in the direction of popular sites. The Center City District—the downtown area—has goodwill ambassadors who are dressed in teal uniforms and equipped with maps to help you navigate the historic city.

A multitude of walking tours are available, from free Park-Ranger-led historical tours to architectural, food-based, ghost, nighttime, and even Ben-Franklin-based tours offered by private tour companies.

DINING AND RECREATION

Philadelphia is known for having authentic cuisine from all over the world. Be sure to try some of the city's famed regional fare, including the famous cheesesteaks, soft pretzels, water ice, hoagies, and fresh seafood.

When dining out, you can BYOB—Bring Your Own Bottle of wine or beer—to a wide variety of designated restaurants. For listings of these BYOB permitting restaurants, visit www.visitphilly.com.

The city has the nation's oldest diamond district on Jewelers Row, plus one of the largest retail shopping complexes in the country. In Pennsylvania, there is no sales tax on clothes or shoes. (See www.discoverphl.com for more information.)

Benjamin Franklin Parkway: This bold diagonal street in the Museum District ends at the Philadelphia Art Museum. The parkway's design was inspired by the Champs-Élysées in Paris.

The region boasts 2,874 cultural attractions, including several hundred historic sites that date back to the Revolution. A number of art and science museums are concentrated in the Parkway Museum District along Benjamin Franklin Parkway.

Many of Philadelphia's most popular sites are free. In Independence National Historical Park, for example, admission is free to the Liberty Bell, Carpenters' Hall, the President's House Site, and Independence Hall.

William Penn chose Philadelphia's location because it was between two rivers where ships could unload their cargo. He thought settlers would build on both rivers and then move to the center. However, settlers preferred the Delaware River, so the city developed from Penn's Landing east to west.

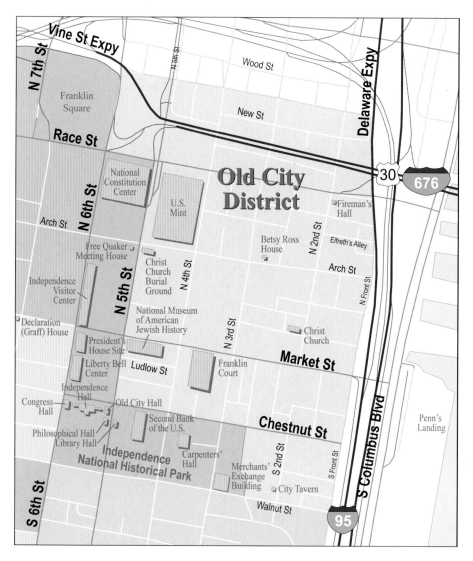

Today, while the public squares that William Penn created have been renamed, they are still an integral part of the city's fabric. Each has its own unique neighborhood: Washington Square is in a quiet, residential neighborhood located near Independence Hall; Franklin Square offers family-friendly activities in the Old City; Rittenhouse Square, west of City Hall, is a popular dining and shopping destination; and Logan Square is located close to the museums along Benjamin Franklin Parkway.

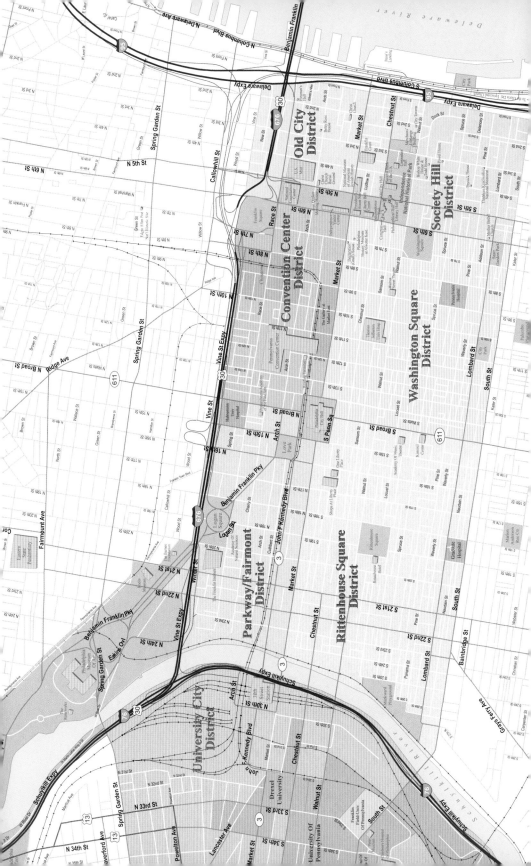

*P*hiladelphia offers a lot to do for everyone. Below are some suggested itineraries that include must-see experiences and famed attractions—many with historical ties to Philadelphia. (Please note that the times listed after each site denote the range for the visit but do not include possible wait times. Estimated times are based on the site and the number of things to see.)

ITINERARY 1:
AMERICA'S MOST HISTORIC SQUARE MILE

To experience Philadelphia's role in early American history, start your visit at the very beginning—in the city's Historic Square Mile, the heart of where the nation was born.

THE PRESIDENT'S HOUSE SITE •
10 TO 30 MINUTES

The mansion that once stood on this site served as an office and residence for presidents George Washington and John Adams. Today, it commemorates the presidents as well as the enslaved Africans who lived and toiled here.

LIBERTY BELL CENTER •
10 TO 30 MINUTES

Housing America's iconic symbol of freedom, the Liberty Bell Center is located between Independence Hall and the Independence Visitor Center. The Liberty Bell Center includes the Liberty Bell, exhibits, and a short film.

INDEPENDENCE HALL •
1 HOUR

The Declaration of Independence and the U.S. Constitution were debated and signed here. Guided tours begin in the East Wing building. Tour tickets must be obtained at the Independence Visitor Center. (This building can be seen by tour only.)

 indicates a National Park Service site

WEST WING OF INDEPENDENCE HALL • 15 MINUTES

The Great Essentials exhibit features surviving copies of the Declaration of Independence, the Articles of Confederation, and the Constitution of the United State. The silver inkstand used to sign these documents is also on display.

CONGRESS HALL • 30 MINUTES

This was the capitol of the United States for 10 years. The House of Representatives met biannually on the first floor, and the Senate on the second floor. Washington and Adams were inaugurated in this building.

OLD CITY HALL • 15 MINUTES

The Supreme Court met biannually in the first floor courtroom during the 10 years that Philadelphia was the national capital. During the 1793 yellow fever epidemic, volunteers met with the mayor here daily to help combat the disease.

DECLARATION HOUSE • 10 TO 20 MINUTES

Thomas Jefferson drafted the Declaration of Independence from his rented rooms on the second floor of this recreated home in June 1776.

NATIONAL CONSTITUTION CENTER • 1 TO 2 HOURS

Built in 2003, this is the first-ever national museum to explain and document the Constitution of the United States. It includes interactive exhibits and a theater with live performances.

PORTRAIT GALLERY IN THE SECOND BANK • 45 MINUTES

This beautiful Greek revival building holds the People of Independence exhibit. Original life portraits by Gilbert Stuart, Thomas Sully, and Charles Willson Peale bring the nation's founders to life.

Carpenters' Hall: Located a block east of Independence Square, Carpenters' Hall is still owned and operated by the Carpenters' Company of Philadelphia.

CARPENTERS' HALL • 15 MINUTES

The First Continental Congress met here in 1774 to petition the British crown for their rights as Englishmen. The hall also is a showcase for 18th century building techniques.

CITY TAVERN • 1 TO 2 HOURS (WHEN DINING)

Called the most genteel tavern in America by John Adams, this fine dining restaurant serves colonial favorites such as West Indies pepper pot soup and turkey potpie in an 18th century atmosphere.

FRANKLIN COURT AND THE BENJAMIN FRANKLIN MUSEUM • 90 MINUTES

Benjamin Franklin lived here while serving in the Continental Congress and the Constitutional Convention. Although his house is long gone, a new state-of-the-art museum under the remaining foundations of the house explores his genius and accomplishments. Along Market Street, there is a working 18th-century style printing office, an archeology exhibit, and a post office.

BETSY ROSS HOUSE • 30 MINUTES

This well-preserved house was the home and workplace of flag maker Betsy Ross. The house has been restored to reflect her life. She is buried in the garden courtyard.

CHRIST CHURCH • 10 TO 20 MINUTES

This church is known as "The Nation's Church" because of the famous Revolutionary-era leaders who worshiped here. George Washington and Betsy Ross sat in the church's pews. Benjamin Franklin's grave is in its burial ground, located just a few blocks from the church.

ELFRETH'S ALLEY • 10 TO 30 MINUTES

Known as the oldest continually inhabited street in the country, Elfreth's Alley includes several homes that are open to the public. The oldest home was built in 1728.

FIREMAN'S HALL MUSEUM • 10 TO 30 MINUTES

Located in a restored 1902 firehouse, this museum—owned by the City of Philadel-phia—highlights moments in Philadelphia firefighting, past and present.

FRANKLIN SQUARE •
1 HOUR

Originally called Northeast Square, Franklin Square was renamed after Benjamin Franklin in 1825. This kid-friendly square, located near the historic district, includes a carousel, miniature golf course, playground, and park.

ITINERARY 2:
ARTS AND CULTURE

After touring the Historic Square Mile, visit some of Philadelphia's other cultural and historic attractions, including the museums along the Benjamin Franklin Parkway. Other sightseeing options include Philadelphia's highest public observation deck at City Hall and the famous "Rocky" steps at the east entrance to the Philadelphia Museum of Art, which offer a sweeping view of the city.

PHILADELPHIA HISTORY MUSEUM AT ATWATER KENT • 1 HOUR

This museum is dedicated to the 300-plus years of history in Philadelphia, from the landing of William Penn in 1682 to the desk George Washington used in Philadelphia while president of the new nation.

NATIONAL MUSEUM OF AMERICAN JEWISH HISTORY • 1 HOUR

Opened in 2010 and located on Independence Mall, this museum documents the American Jewish experience. It is the only museum in the nation dedicated to collecting, preserving, and interpreting American Jewish artifacts. There are more than 10,000 items.

CITY HALL AND TOWER TOUR • 1 HOUR

Located in William Penn's Center Square, City Hall houses the mayor's office and other city offices. The tower is the tallest masonry support structure in the world. The observation deck on the tower offers a 360-degree view of Philadelphia and is the highest public observation deck in the city.

PENNSYLVANIA ACADEMY OF THE FINE ARTS • 1 HOUR

Founded in 1805, the Pennsylvania Academy of the Fine Arts (PAFA) is the nation's first school of fine arts and museum. It is known for its collection of 19th and 20th century American art.

BENJAMIN FRANKLIN PARKWAY • 5 TO 8 HOURS

The Benjamin Franklin Parkway in the Museum District is home to world-class museums and institutions, which include the Academy of Natural Sciences of Drexel University, America's oldest natural sciences museum; the Franklin Institute, one of the first hands-on science museums in the country; the Barnes Foundation with its unparalleled collection of impressionist paintings; the Fairmount Water Works, one of Philadelphia's legendary landmarks; and the Philadelphia Museum of Art with its famous "Rocky" steps and statue.

EASTERN STATE PENITENTIARY • 90 MINUTES

The world's first penitentiary dates from the 19th century. Although it has been closed for years, this massive building now includes tours—and a way out.

ITINERARY 3: VENTURE OUT

Philadelphia is full of interesting and unique neighborhoods with parks, shopping, and dining. Next, try exploring Rittenhouse Square, University City, the Philadelphia Zoo, and Philadelphia's many other attractions.

READING TERMINAL MARKET • 1 HOUR

The Reading Terminal Market, the nation's oldest continuously open farmers' market, features a variety of regional food vendors and restaurants.

LOVE PARK AND SISTER CITIES PARK • 30 MINUTES

LOVE Park was dedicated as John F. Kennedy Plaza in 1967. The nickname "LOVE Park" comes from the iconic LOVE sculpture by artist Robert Indiana on 15th Street and John F. Kennedy Blvd. Sister Cities Park on Benjamin Franklin Parkway is named for President Eisenhower's vision of connecting communities to foster a more peaceful world. Philadelphia's sister cities include Florence, Italy; Tel Aviv, Israel; and Kobe, Japan.

KELLY DRIVE • 1 HOUR

This four-mile stretch of park is named after John B. Kelly Jr., brother of famous actress and Princess of Monaco, Grace Kelly. It runs along the Schuylkill River and is home to the nation's oldest collegiate boat race, the Dad Vail Regatta.

LOVE Park: Robert Indiana's famous sculpture in LOVE Park was installed for the nation's 1976 bicentennial.

Philadelphia Zoo: Known as America's first zoo, the Philadelphia Zoo is located on the banks of the Schuylkill River. Its famous Victorian gates and gatehouse were built for the zoo's opening day in 1874.

CHINATOWN • 1 HOUR
Established in 1890, Philadelphia's Chinatown is home to the first authentic Chinese gate built outside of China. There are numerous restaurants and shops.

RITTENHOUSE SQUARE • 2 HOURS
Named after David Rittenhouse, astronomer and first director of the U.S. Mint, Rittenhouse Square is a hub of high end dining and shopping.

PHILADELPHIA ZOO • 2 HOURS
The nation's oldest zoo, which was established in 1859, features more than 1,300 animals, many of them rare and endangered.

UNIVERSITY CITY/ UNIVERSITY OF PENNSYLVANIA MUSEUM OF ARCHAEOLOGY AND ANTHROPOLOGY (PENN MUSEUM) • 2 HOURS
This West Philadelphia neighborhood is named for the universities and colleges in the area. There are a wide variety of restaurants, coffee shops, and tree-lined campus walks. The Penn Museum features Egyptian mummies, Chinese dragon sculptures, and gold from the Middle East and Peru.

PENN'S LANDING • 2 HOURS
This stretch of waterfront along the Delaware River is the site where William Penn arrived in Philadelphia on his ship, the *Welcome*. It is also home to restaurants and the Independence Seaport Museum.

Early Pennsylvania History

The area now known as Pennsylvania was first inhabited 15,000 years ago by indigenous peoples. Much later, Europeans settled in the area, attracted by its fertile soil, densely wooded hills, and bountiful rivers. In 1638, the Swedes arrived on the *Kalmer Nickel*, a Dutch ship. Their first settlement, in 1643, was on Tinicum Island, near today's Philadelphia International Airport. Soon afterward, the Swedes founded the town of Upland (now Chester, Pennsylvania) to the south. Settlements in the colony of New Sweden stretched along both sides of the Delaware River—from Cape May, New Jersey, to Trenton, New Jersey, and inland to Reading, Pennsylvania. The Swedish colonists practiced agriculture and traded for furs with the local Lenape Indians.

Kalmer Nickel: In 1638, the Swedish ship *Kalmer Nickel* brought 24 settlers to America after a two-month Atlantic crossing.

New Sweden was not secure, though: The Dutch claimed the entire region as part of New Amsterdam. As the Swedes built settlements, Dutch settlers began increasing their fur trade with the Lenape. In 1655, the Dutch conquered New Sweden with a fleet of seven ships and 300 soldiers.

Nine years later, British troops seized the entire mid-Atlantic region in the name of the Duke of York (later King James II of England). The Duke of York granted land to two friends, Sir George Carteret and Lord Berkeley of Stratton, who called their colony New Jersey. The duke kept the northern section and renamed it New York in his own honor. Present-day Pennsylvania and Delaware remained under the duke's jurisdiction until 1681. At that time, the duke's older brother, England's King Charles II, deeded the land to William Penn.

William Penn: This 1834 portrait by Henry Inman shows Penn holding the charter for Pennsylvania. As a humble Quaker, Penn named his colony Sylvania, or "Woods." The king changed it to "Pennsylvania" in honor of Penn's father.

QUAKER BEGINNINGS

William Penn was born in England in 1644 into an aristocratic family. His father, Admiral Sir William Penn, was a friend and supporter of King Charles II. When the younger Penn was 22, he denounced the Anglican Church—the official Church of England—and became a Quaker, a member of the Religious Society of Friends.

Penn's Writings: William Penn was a skilled writer on many topics, especially his Quaker faith. This formal letter, *William Penn's Last Farewell to England*, was written before Penn journeyed to the New World. It commended the Quakers for their faithfulness.

George Fox: Penn became a great friend of George Fox, founder of the Religious Society of Friends, or the Quakers. Penn and Fox often traveled together to preach.

The society was founded around 1650 in England. Quakers, who believed that God speaks directly to each person, did not agree with the concept of a "hireling ministry" or church hierarchy. This put them at odds with the official (Anglican) Church of England. They also did not bow or doff their hats to those in authority, since they believed that all men and women were equal in the eyes of God. Quakers advocated nonviolence, simplicity in speech and dress, and moderation in eating and drinking. They refused to take oaths of any kind—even loyalty oaths to the king. For their beliefs, they suffered imprisonment and deportation.

Penn was arrested and imprisoned in the Tower of London several times. He wrote many tracts in defense of his Quaker faith, some while he was in prison. In 1670, when Penn's father died, he left his son a fortune and an outstanding loan of £16,000 that the king owed to his family. In settlement of this debt, King Charles II deeded to Penn a significant grant of land in 1681—45,000 square miles of land in the middle of the British colonies.

A REFUGE OF RELIGIOUS FREEDOM

Penn's colony, roughly the size of England, stretched along the Delaware River and included present-day Pennsylvania and Delaware. As the ruler and landlord, or proprietor, of Pennsylvania, Penn could govern as he wished. The restrictions on his grant simply required that the laws he instituted be in harmony with those of England and be agreed upon by a representative assembly.

> *"You are now fixed at the mercy of no governor that comes to make his fortune great; you shall be governed by laws of your own making and live a free, and if you will, a sober and industrious life."*
>
> — William Penn, in a letter to those already residing in Pennsylvania, 1681

For William Penn, the grant was an opportunity to try a "holy experiment." He decided his province would serve as a refuge—a place of religious freedom and almost total self-government. (He later codified this in his 1701 Charter of Privileges.) Penn advertised his colony throughout Europe, offering 100 acres for 40 shillings. His promise of refuge appealed to other religious nonconformists, including Amish people, Mennonites, Moravians, and Baptists, as well as Catholics, Huguenots, and Jews.

Within two years, more than 3,000 settlers had arrived in Pennsylvania, many of them English, Welsh, Scots, Scots-Irish, and German. Large numbers of Welsh Quakers settled in Philadelphia and just west of the city, and numerous German immigrants traveled up the Schuylkill and Perkiomen river valleys to settle in what is today Allentown. By 1730, 4,000 enslaved Africans also lived in Pennsylvania, including some that had belonged to William Penn.

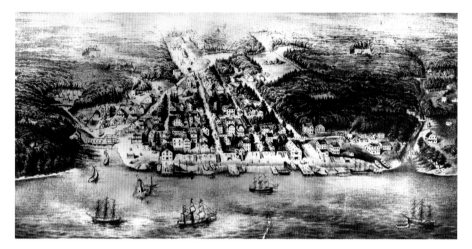

City Location: Sketches like these were used to recruit new settlers to the colony since they showed the advantages of the city's location. There was plenty of wood for building, well-planned streets, and a wide river for transportation.

PLANNING PHILADELPHIA

Penn himself arrived in the colony in 1682. Soon after, he founded a capital city at the convergence of the Delaware and Schuylkill rivers and called it Philadelphia, the City of Brotherly Love. He then spent the winter at Upland, the region's largest settlement, renaming it Chester.

Penn, who had seen London devastated by the 1665 bubonic plague and the Great Fire of 1666, wished to create "a greene Country Towne. Which will never be burnt and always be wholesome." Working with his land surveyor, Thomas Holme, Penn laid out a capital city with wide, straight streets and large lots. Philadelphia was planned with a central square surrounded by four other squares. Following the Quaker custom of not naming places after people, he called them Centre Square and Northeast, Northwest, Southeast, and Southwest squares. (The squares have since been named for Washington and famous Philadelphians.) Each square featured large green public spaces surrounded by house lots large enough for families to have their own gardens.

Map of Greater Philadelphia: In the 18th century, travel by water was faster and more comfortable than by land. Philadelphia's location on the Delaware River offered a safe and convenient harbor.

Philadelphia was, as Penn had hoped, a great marriage of city and country life, a capital city with both urban amenities and open space. Well situated and well planned, the city grew rapidly, attracting many skilled artisans and tradesmen. Within two years, it had more than 600 homes, many of them handsome brick row houses. By the time the First Continental Congress convened there in 1774, Philadelphia was the largest and most cosmopolitan metropolis in British North America.

PENN AND THE NATIVE AMERICANS

When the English arrived in Pennsylvania, they settled in lands that were mostly vacated by the native population due to the recent "Beaver Wars." Penn hoped for peace and harmony with the area's remaining Native Americans. Before arriving in the New World, he sent gifts to the Lenape Indians and learned several Indian dialects to be able to negotiate with them. He also introduced laws that gave native peoples a fair trial in disputes with European settlers, promising an equal number of people from both groups on the jury. The "Great Treaty" of Shackamaxon was Penn's most famous treaty with the Lenape, memorialized by Benjamin West's 1771 painting of the subject. However, he excluded native people from citizenship.

> "We meet on the broad pathway of good faith and good-will; no advantage shall be taken on either side, but all shall be openness and love."
>
> — William Penn, in his "Great Treaty" with the Indians at Shackamaxon, 1683

Penn's policy of peaceful coexistence with the native population was pursued during the colony's first 60 years, when the Quakers held power in Pennsylvania. But there were strains, especially after the infamous 1737 "Walking Purchase" carried out by Penn's sons. While Penn had made it a point to compensate native Indians fairly in land transactions, he had not been careful with his own fortune and had died in debt. To gain more land, Penn's sons purposely misinterpreted the terms of the Walking Purchase. Actions like this and the push of European settlers westward created increasing friction between the settlers and native tribes.

William Penn's Treaty with the Indians: Commissioned by William Penn's son Thomas, American artist Benjamin West painted this piece in London in 1771, almost 100 years after the actual meeting under the "Treaty Elm."

The Landing of William Penn: Lenape Indians and Swedish settlers greet Penn in Jean L. G. Ferris's 1900 painting.

REVOLUTIONARY PRINCIPLES

William Penn's "holy experiment" made Pennsylvania the most religiously tolerant and ethnically diverse colony in the New World. He set forth principles of religious freedom, democracy, fair trials, and humane sentencing, and he reduced the number of capital crimes to only two: treason and murder. Many of these principles were also drafted into the Declaration of Independence and the U.S. Constitution. These documents would be written in Penn's capital city of Philadelphia during the American Revolution nearly 100 years later.

The Pennsylvania State House in Philadelphia: Construction on this building was started in 1732, the same year George Washington was born and Benjamin Franklin first published *Poor Richard's Almanack.*

THE WAR FOR INDEPENDENCE

The American Revolution was an event of sweeping worldwide importance. More than just a battle for freedom, the war presented the revolutionary idea that governments should exist for the benefit of the people governed. Yet the fight was costly: It took eight years for the colonies to secure America's independence and give their democratic form of government the chance to continue.

At its core, the Revolutionary War pitted American colonists, who wanted "no taxation without representation" and full rights as English citizens, against the power of the British crown to rule its colony. But the war was not just waged against an outside authority. At certain times, American Patriots fought American Loyalists as in a civil war. From the family whose farm was raided, to the merchant who was unable to trade, to the enslaved African who fought along British lines on the promise of freedom, everyone had a stake in the outcome.

Map of the 13 Colonies: The seacoast and rivers are clearly marked on this map, since these bodies of water were used to easily transport goods and people. The few inland roads were rough and usually made of dirt or mud.

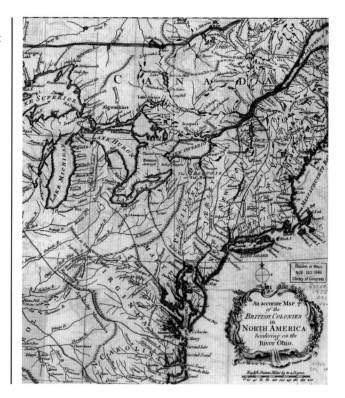

APPROACH TO WAR

Between 1607 and 1733, the British Empire established 13 colonies along the Atlantic coast of North America. These colonies—Massachusetts, New Hampshire, New York, Connecticut, Rhode Island, Pennsylvania, New Jersey, Delaware, Maryland, Virginia, North Carolina, South Carolina, and Georgia—developed their own forms of self-government under the jurisdiction of the British crown.

> *"Is life so dear, or peace so sweet, as to be purchased at the price of chains and slavery? Forbid it, Almighty God! I know not what course others may take; but as for me, give me liberty or give me death!"*
>
> — Patrick Henry, March 23, 1775

For the majority of American colonists, the seeds of discontent grew slowly. Most were of British ancestry; they traded with Great Britain and shared Britain's Protestant religious tradition. The colonists' loyalty to the crown reached a high point in 1763, after Britain's victory in the French and Indian War. Britain gained all of French Canada and the territory east of the Mississippi River, including Spanish Florida. However, the peace treaty proclaimed that no British settlements could be established west of the Allegheny Mountains. This restricted access to the fertile Ohio Valley. The war also left Britain with huge debts.

To secure her new possessions, Britain kept an army in America—and looked to the colonies to help pay for it. Many colonists were upset with Britain's decision to keep an army in America. Almost all of them opposed Parliament's effort to raise taxes without colonial representation. Over the next decade, the British Parliament began to impose higher taxes and stricter laws. These measures brought strong protests, which spurred Parliament to clamp down harder. For the Americans, this increasing friction would explode into fiery outrage by 1775.

ACTS OF PROTEST

The hostilities began in 1765, two years after Britain's victory in the French and Indian War. Parliament passed the Stamp Act, which taxed the sale of playing cards, dice, newspapers, and legal documents. The colonists resisted, insisting that Parliament could not tax them: British subjects could only be taxed with the consent of their elected representatives, and the colonies had no representation in the House of Commons.

The colonists organized a successful nonimportation movement. This action, along with colonial agent Benjamin Franklin's eloquence in London, persuaded Parliament to repeal the Stamp Act in March 1766. The same day, Parliament passed the Declaratory Act, which affirmed its complete authority over the colonies "in all cases whatsoever." Opposition continued to grow. The colonies created Committees of Correspondence to share information, and the colonial press eagerly reported the news from other colonies. In 1770, British soldiers in Boston fired into an angry mob of protesters, leaving five dead. The incident, known as the Boston Massacre, was the first bloodshed in the American Revolution.

> "If taxes are laid upon us in any shape without ever having a legal representation where they are laid, are we not reduced from the character of free subjects to the miserable state of tributary slaves?"
>
> — Excerpts from a Boston town meeting, May 24, 1764

In 1773, Parliament passed the Tea Act, giving the British East India Company a monopoly in the tea trade. That December, a crowd of about 100 colonists thinly disguised as Indians stormed the trading ships and had a "Tea Party," dumping tea into Boston Harbor. In response, Parliament passed the so-called "Intolerable Acts." These acts placed Massachusetts under military rule and required colonists to house British officers in their homes. Britain also closed the port of Boston to any trade until the East India Company was paid for the expensive tea.

Boston Tea Party: On December 16, 1773, Patriots took action to protest the tea tax and the British monopoly on tea by dumping tea into Boston Harbor. In New York and Philadelphia, protesters succeeded in preventing the imported tea from being sold.

Ladies Boycotting Tea: This 1775 British cartoon mocks the 51 women of Edenton, North Carolina, who signed a 1774 petition against the tea tax. Women were not expected to take so public an action.

To coordinate support for Massachusetts and opposition to the Intolerable Acts, the colonies sent delegates to a Continental Congress in Philadelphia in September 1774. The delegates drafted a Declaration of Resolves, agreed to boycotts if needed for repeal, established Committees of Correspondence, and petitioned the king for help. They set a second meeting for May 1775. While they were still loyal to the king, the delegates wanted the full rights of English citizens.

OUTBREAK OF WAR

While Parliament considered the colonists' demands, the fighting began. On April 19, 1775, British troops left Boston to seize military supplies and encountered colonial militia and minutemen blocking their way. Shots rang out at Lexington and the North Bridge at Concord. It was the first clash in the Revolutionary War—"the shot heard round the world," as Ralph Waldo Emerson later wrote.

The First Resistance: This 1911 painting by E. Percy Moran depicts the Americans' first skirmish with the British. Moran, from a prominent family of artists, studied at the Pennsylvania Academy of the Fine Arts.

As news of the fighting spread, thousands of volunteer soldiers rushed to a makeshift camp in Cambridge, Massachusetts. Soon the American troops had bottled up the British army in Boston. Other colonial forces took the British forts at Ticonderoga and Crown Point in New York, seizing valuable cannon and other military supplies.

British Cannon: Both the Continental Army and the British Army used cannon like this one during artillery battles.

Continental Army: At the beginning of the war, few soldiers had regulation uniforms like the ones shown in this illustration.

Less than a month later, on May 10, 1775, a Second Continental Congress convened in Philadelphia at the Pennsylvania State House to discuss the growing hostilities. The delegates named John Hancock of Massachusetts as the presiding officer, and John Adams proposed that George Washington of Virginia command the Continental Army. Washington was quickly approved and left for Massachusetts.

The Second Continental Congress spent the summer debating the best course of action. In July 1775, the delegates sent King George III the Olive Branch Petition, urging the king to end the fighting and return to peace. King George refused the colonists' petition. The colonies, he declared, were in open rebellion.

> *"If we wish to be free, if we mean to preserve inviolate those inestimable privileges for which we have been so long contending, if we mean not basely to abandon the noble struggle in which we have been so long engaged... we must fight!"*

— Patrick Henry, speaking to the convention of delegates in Virginia, March 23, 1775

IN THE ARMY NOW

When George Washington took charge of the Continental Army in 1775, he faced enormous challenges. Unlike the British army, the American troops were inexperienced, unorganized, and poorly equipped. From this raw group of colonists, Washington began to mold a fighting force that would eventually win the war for independence.

The soldiers who fought were a diverse group. Some were born in the colonies, while others were immigrants. They were rich and poor, free and enslaved, Protestant and "Fighting" Quaker. Many of the Continentals were New Englanders; large numbers of colonists, especially in New York and Georgia, were Loyalists who fought with the British.

An estimated 5,000 African Americans actively fought for the Americans. Many more sided with the British, who promised them freedom in exchange for their services. Though fewer than 1,000 enslaved Africans served as British soldiers, tens of thousands sought freedom by serving as cooks, nurses, teamsters, and laborers for the British army. About 20,000 received their freedom at the end of the war and were evacuated with the British, including some of George Washington's enslaved people. But thousands were left behind and returned to bondage.

Native Americans also fought on both sides. In the northern colonies, the Oneidas and Tuscaroras sided with the Americans, participating in scouting and harassment operations. The Mohawks, led by Joseph Brant, stayed loyal to the British, and most Cayugas, Onondagas, and Senecas joined them. They knew an American victory would increase the tide of settlers on their tribal lands. In the end, however, it didn't matter where the Native Americans fought. They eventually lost all of their land as settlers moved westward after the war.

THE WAR'S EARLY STAGES

Two months after Lexington and Concord, on June 17, 1775, the Battle of Bunker Hill occurred. There, on Breed's Hill, inexperienced colonial soldiers held off British regulars for more than two hours. The Patriots were forced to abandon their position, including the high ground of Bunker Hill overlooking Boston, but the British suffered heavy losses: Of their 2,200 soldiers, more than 1,000 ended up dead or wounded.

Battle of Bunker Hill: Although the well-equipped and experienced British troops technically won the Battle of Bunker Hill, they suffered heavy losses. The battle proved to the raw American troops that they could hold their own in a pitched battle.

In August 1775, with American and British troops stalemated in Boston, Washington sent some of his troops north to take Canada. Led by major generals Benedict Arnold and Richard Montgomery, the Canada campaign was Washington's first major military offensive. The American troops attacked Quebec on December 30, 1775, and the battle ended in bitter defeat for the Patriots. The Continental Army retreated from Canada in 1776. Canada never joined the rebellion against Britain.

The Continental troops near Boston were more successful. In late March 1776, under Colonel Henry Knox, the Continental Army brought the last of the 55 cannon from Fort Ticonderoga to the siege at Boston. The resulting cannon fire forced the British out of Boston.

In June, American forces repulsed an all-day British naval attack on Sullivan's Island in Charleston, South Carolina. Due to the tricky waters of Charleston Harbor and the Patriots' resistance, South Carolina remained untouched by the British for three more years.

British Ship in Charleston Harbor: Powered by sails rather than engines, navy ships were significantly affected by the wind and tides.

COMMON SENSE

In 1775, despite the growing turmoil, Congress could not agree on whether to formally separate from Great Britain. Many delegates still considered themselves loyal British subjects who simply wanted the same rights as those living in Britain. In addition, many people in the colonies were Loyalists, satisfied with British rule.

The turning point in public opinion came in January 1776 with the publication of *Common Sense*, a pamphlet written in Philadelphia by a newly arrived Englishman named Thomas Paine. The pamphlet argued that the time had come for the colonists to make a complete break with England. Their liberty would never be safe while Britain governed them, because England's government adhered to monarchy and hereditary rule. Paine urged Americans to create a new form of government—a modern republic—based entirely on popular consent.

> *"These are the times that try men's souls. . . . Tyranny, like hell, is not easily conquered; yet we have this consolation with us, that the harder the conflict, the more glorious the triumph."*
>
> — Thomas Paine, *The American Crisis*, December 23, 1776

Common Sense created a furor. Within a few months, 200,000 copies were in circulation, and the revolutionary movement had won thousands of new converts. Capitalizing on this popular support, Richard Henry Lee of Virginia put forth a resolution on June 7, 1776, urging Congress to declare independence from England. The delegates remained divided, though, so they postponed further discussion of the resolution for a few weeks.

THE DECLARATION OF INDEPENDENCE

In the meantime, Congress appointed a committee to draft a declaration stating why the American colonies were entitled to form an independent nation. The committee consisted of five delegates: Thomas Jefferson, Benjamin Franklin, John Adams, Robert Livingston, and Roger Sherman. Written primarily by Thomas Jefferson in his rented Philadelphia rooms, the document included three parts: reasons America should sever ties with Great Britain, a list of wrongdoings the king had committed against America, and the statement that America was now an independent nation.

Edited out were comments critical of slavery. The document's famous words read in part: "We hold these truths to be self-evident, that all men are created equal, that they are endowed by their Creator with certain unalienable Rights, that among these are Life, Liberty and the pursuit of Happiness. That to secure these rights, Governments are instituted among Men, deriving their just powers from the consent of the Governed, that whenever any Form of Government becomes destructive of these ends, it is the Right of the People to alter or abolish it, and to institute new Government."

> *"That these United Colonies are, and of right ought to be, free and independent States, that they are absolved from all allegiance to the British Crown, and that all political connection between them and the State of Great Britain is, and ought to be, totally dissolved."*
>
> — Richard Henry Lee, the Resolution of Independence, June 7, 1776

Jefferson's eloquent words turned the colonists' specific complaints about representation, taxes, and the subversion of the legal system into an assertion that all governments had a universal duty to protect the rights of their citizens. On July 4, 1776—a full year after the fighting had begun at Lexington and Concord—the delegates adopted the Declaration of Independence.

FOUNDING FATHERS

Most of the 56 delegates who affixed their names to the Declaration did so during a ceremony on August 2, 1776. They were a distinguished group. Though socially diverse, most were well educated and prosperous. In terms of wealth, they ranged from Samuel Adams (Massachusetts), whose friends supplied money and clothes so he could attend Congress, to planter Charles Carroll (Maryland), one of the richest men in America. The youngest signer was 26-year-old Edward Rutledge (South Carolina); the oldest was 70-year-old Benjamin Franklin (Pennsylvania).

The Declaration of Independence: Thomas Jefferson and the committee present the draft of the Declaration of Independence to John Hancock in this painting by John Trumbull. The original signed version of the Declaration was never sent to King George; he received a printed, unsigned copy.

More than half of the delegates were lawyers, such as John Adams (Massachusetts) and James Wilson (Pennsylvania). Some were merchants and shippers, such as John Hancock (Massachusetts). Four were doctors, including Josiah Bartlett (New Hampshire), and four were trained as ministers like John Witherspoon (New Jersey). Many from the south were farmers with large plantations worked by enslaved labor, including George Washington (Virginia) and John Rutledge (South Carolina). The majority of the signers owned enslaved servants at one time or another.

Drafting the Declaration of Independence: This 19th century print shows the five members of the committee appointed to draft the Declaration of Independence. They are (from left to right): Robert Livingston of New York, John Adams of Massachusetts, Benjamin Franklin of Pennsylvania, Roger Sherman of Connecticut, and seated in front, Thomas Jefferson of Virginia. Most of the text was drafted by Jefferson with a few suggestions by Franklin. It was approved on July 4, 1776.

Almost all the signers emerged poorer for their years of public service and resulting neglect of their personal affairs. Many like Elbridge Gerry (Massachusetts) saw their businesses deteriorate as a result of embargoes on trade with Britain. A number of farmers, such as William Floyd (New York) and John Hart (New Jersey), had their lands destroyed by British troops. Several—including Robert Morris (Pennsylvania)—loaned money to the government, which was not repaid for a long time. About one-third of the group served as militia officers, including Oliver Wolcott (Connecticut), with most seeing battlefield action, and five of the delegates were taken captive, including Edward Rutledge (South Carolina). The homes of nearly one-third of the signers were destroyed or damaged, like Benjamin Franklin's Philadelphia home.

For their dedication to the cause of independence, the men who signed the Declaration of Independence risked loss of fortune, imprisonment, and death.

THE ARTICLES OF CONFEDERATION

At the same time that Richard Henry Lee urged a resolution for independence, he also proposed that "a plan of confederation be prepared and transmitted to the respective colonies for their consideration." Therefore, while Thomas Jefferson was writing the Declaration of Independence, Congress began work on a national government. One delegate from each colony served on a committee to discuss the confederation, and John Dickinson of Philadelphia was chosen to draft the document.

> "But I find, although the colonies have differed in religion, laws, customs, and manners, yet in the great essentials of society and government they are all alike."
>
> — John Adams to Abigail Adams, July 10, 1776

The resulting document became the Articles of Confederation. The Articles were a union of sovereign states that issued their own currency, collected import duties, and even raised their own navies. The central government took care of foreign affairs but could not collect taxes. Each state had one vote in the central government. The delegates adopted the Articles of Confederation in late 1777, but it took until 1781 for all 13 states to ratify them.

The Articles of Confederation: The Articles were a union of sovereign states with a central government. This government passed the Northwest Ordinance, which enabled newly settled territories to become states and laid the foundation for westward expansion.

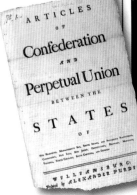

Silver Inkstand: This is the actual ceremonial inkstand (cast in 1752 by Phillip Syng) that the signers of the Declaration and U.S. Constitution used to sign the documents. It is on view in the West Wing of Independence Hall.

SUPPORT FOR THE CAUSE

Once the delegates to the Continental Congress made the decision to formally separate from Great Britain and had issued the Declaration of Independence, they turned their attention to fighting the war and building a new nation. Raising money to pay for the Continental Army—which lacked basic supplies, uniforms, and shoes—was one task. Washington also needed funds to retain the thousands of soldiers whose enlistments were soon to expire. To seek resources and alliances for the new nation, Congress sent Benjamin Franklin to France, John Adams to Holland, and Arthur Lee to Spain.

In the meantime, General Washington worked to boost the morale of the troops. On Christmas night in 1776, he moved them from Pennsylvania to New Jersey to prepare for attack. Leading the army across the icy Delaware River was a dangerous challenge. Not all of Washington's generals supported the plan. The following morning, though, Washington's troops surprised—and defeated—the German Hessian troops fighting for Britain at Trenton. They achieved a similar victory over British troops at Princeton on January 3. With these victories, the colonists began to believe that they just might win the war.

Washington Crossing the Delaware: This 1851 painting by Emanuel Leutze captures George Washington's bold move on Christmas night to cross the Delaware River and attack the British in New Jersey, which surprised the enemy and inspired Americans.

THE PHILADELPHIA CAMPAIGN

In 1777, General Howe of Britain instituted a two-pronged attack against the Americans. First, he tried to isolate radical New England from the other colonies—and invoke the support of silent Loyalists—by sending a force from Canada to the Hudson River. Then he sent troops from New York City toward the capital of Philadelphia.

General Howe's reasons for attacking Philadelphia were numerous: Philadelphia was the largest city in British North America and the seat of the American government. It had a number of prominent Loyalists, it was part of a fertile region, and it could be supplied from the sea using the Delaware River. Furthermore, Howe believed the attack would occupy General Washington and would force his surrender.

> "Rebellion to tyrants is obedience to God."
>
> — Thomas Jefferson's favorite motto, used on his personal seal

Washington spent most of the spring and summer of 1777 moving through New Jersey to guard the capital at Philadelphia and to prevent Howe from traveling up the Hudson River near New York. Meanwhile, Howe moved his troops by sea to the head of Chesapeake Bay below Philadelphia. Washington marched south and met him at Brandywine Creek, southwest of Philadelphia, on September 11, 1777. Outflanked by the British, the Americans were forced to retreat.

On September 26, the British marched into Philadelphia unopposed. They stationed 9,000 troops in Germantown, a small village a few miles northwest of Philadelphia, and left the rest of the troops to occupy the city. With the British troops divided, General Washington prepared a surprise attack on Germantown early on the morning of October 4.

Washington's battle plan was thrown into disarray in the fog and smoke. The main action took place along Germantown Pike at the large stone mansion called Cliveden and farther south at Market Square. Howe made his headquarters in a stone house across from the market. The British won the day, and the Continental Army fled to spend the winter in Valley Forge. With no troops left to defend it, Philadelphia had officially fallen to the crown.

Cliveden: This stone house, located at 6401 Germantown Avenue, survived the Battle of Germantown despite a fierce attack by American troops on the British soldiers inside.

UNDER BRITISH RULE

The capture of Philadelphia forced the Continental Congress to relocate west to York, Pennsylvania, from September 1777 to June 1778. Anticipating the British troops' arrival, many Patriots and businessmen abandoned Philadelphia. In addition, the Continental Army took supplies and any other items that might be useful to the British, such as large metal bells. Those residents who remained were a mixture of Loyalists, neutral Quakers, and the poor.

During the occupation, the British officers quartered in the city's finest houses, including Benjamin Franklin's. General Howe stayed in a brick mansion at 6th and Market streets. (The home, which was later owned by Robert Morris, became the President's House in the 1790s.) Churches were used as hospitals for wounded soldiers. The Walnut Street Jail housed American prisoners of war. And the State House was used first as quarters for British troops and later for wounded American officers who were taken prisoner.

Walnut Street Jail: Conditions were grim for the American soldiers held here, right, with food and fuel in short supply. Those who died were buried nearby in what is now Washington Square. The jail has since been demolished.

Fort Mifflin: Completed in 1776 under Benjamin Franklin's direction, Fort Mifflin was a strategic fort for the Continental Army.

The Continental Army tried to keep supplies from coming into Philadelphia via the Delaware River. Continental soldiers hid wooden stakes in the middle of the river and reinforced their positions along the river south of the city. After a month of intense bombardment, the British captured Fort Mifflin (near today's Philadelphia Airport). In addition, a Loyalist carpenter pointed out the hidden stakes in the river, enabling the British supply ships to make it up the Delaware and into Philadelphia. For most people in the city, though, food and firewood were expensive and in short supply.

Since armies in the 18th century did not usually fight during the winter, the British officers filled their time in Philadelphia with pleasant diversions. They were welcomed into the homes of the prosperous Loyalists. Just before they evacuated Philadelphia in the spring, the officers gave a lavish ball called the Meschianza in honor of their departing General Howe.

A Changing Battle

Although the British had captured New York City and then Philadelphia, their plan to bring troops south from Montreal to link with Howe's troops was not successful. On October 17, 1777, British General John Burgoyne surrendered his 6,000 troops to American General Horatio Gates at Saratoga, New York. This major victory enabled the American diplomats at the French court—led by Benjamin Franklin—to negotiate an alliance with France in February 1778. The alliance brought financial and military aid that greatly increased the colonists' chances of victory. The new French ambassador, Conrad Alexandre Gerard, was welcomed upon his arrival in Philadelphia. Charles Willson Peale painted his portrait, which now hangs in the Second Bank Portrait Gallery.

During the winter of 1777 to 1778, the Continental troops were stationed at Valley Forge. There, they built cabins, roads, and earthen defense lines and purchased food, clothing, and supplies from surrounding farms. In February 1778, an energetic former Prussian army officer, Baron Friedrich von Steuben, arrived at Valley Forge. With the new drills instituted by von Steuben, the Continental Army emerged as a more effective fighting force.

Valley Forge: Leading daily drills all winter, Baron Friedrich von Steuben helped American soldiers acquire the skills they needed to become an effective army.

The year also brought a major change in the royal army's strategy. Britain had failed to subdue New England, and the war was stalemated in Pennsylvania. Worried about being trapped in Philadelphia by French warships blockading the Delaware River, the British left to defend New York.

THE SOUTHERN CAMPAIGN

Following France's entry into the war, Britain decided to concentrate on subduing the southern colonies. British General Lord Charles Cornwallis led the campaign, which was crafted to incite Patriot fears of slave revolts. After two years, in May 1780, the British army took Charleston, South Carolina.

Charleston was a serious loss for the Americans, but it stirred up resistance. The British army established forts but could not maintain control of the countryside. Once the British troops moved on, the Loyalist troops were at the mercy of their pro-independence neighbors. In October 1780, Patriot militia defeated Loyalist troops at Kings Mountain, South Carolina, ending Loyalist military efforts there.

THE END IN SIGHT

In early 1781, American General Nathanael Greene plotted a strategy to wear down British troops in the south with both hit-and-run tactics and set-piece battles. Although the British won many engagements with the Americans over the next eight months, it was a costly campaign for the royal troops.

> *"Posterity! you will never know how much it cost the present generation to preserve your freedom! I hope you will make a good use of it. If you do not, I shall repent in Heaven that ever I took half the pains to preserve it."*
>
> — John Adams, in a letter to Abigail Adams, April 27, 1777

Meanwhile, the French army arrived in Rhode Island with fresh troops and hard currency. In the spring of 1781, General Jean-Baptiste Rochambeau met with Washington to coordinate a march south with the American troops. Bypassing the British, who were occupying New York City, the two armies made their way through New Jersey. They arrived in Philadelphia in early September. Both armies paraded past the State House as the Continental Congress and the French ambassador reviewed the troops.

The combined troops reached northern Virginia in October. They were aided when the French navy, under Admiral de Grasse, arrived in the Chesapeake Bay and defeated the British navy. With the English fleet departing for New York, the British army was trapped in Yorktown, Virginia. On October 19, 1781, the British troops under General Cornwallis surrendered to the American and French forces. The captured British battle flags were carried to Congress in Philadelphia. There, citizens celebrated the surrender with bonfires and illuminations.

British Troops Surrender at Yorktown: General Cornwallis sent General O'Hara to surrender for the British, so Washington sent General Benjamin Lincoln to accept the surrender.

TREATY OF PARIS

Yorktown was a great victory for the French and American forces, but the war was not over. The British still occupied New York City and various cities in the south, and there was no hope that the Americans would take those cities anytime soon.

England had been worn down by years of war, though, and the British public was no longer willing to pay taxes to support the effort. In 1782, Parliament entered into peace negotiations in Paris. Benjamin Franklin, John Adams, and John Jay represented the Americans. France and Spain were also parties to the treaty.

When it was finally signed in September 1783, the Treaty of Paris officially ended the hostilities, recognized American independence, and made the Mississippi River the new nation's western border. It allowed Britain to retain Canada and returned Florida to Spain. More negotiations and another war with England (from 1812 to 1815) would be necessary to secure the nation, but American independence, virtually unthinkable in 1763, had been achieved.

Treaty of Paris: At the signing ceremony, Benjamin Franklin (standing) wore the same formal suit that he had donned nine years before when he had been viciously insulted by British officials in London.

CONSEQUENCES OF THE WAR

The end of the Revolutionary War brought independence for 13 American states. How Americans would use their newfound freedom, however, was not immediately certain. In 1782, the Loyalists began to evacuate the country. Largely unwelcome in the new United States, about 100,000 found new lives in Britain, Canada, and various British colonies in the West Indies.

Loyalists at Home: Those Loyalists who remained in America had to demonstrate their allegiance to the United States by signing documents and pledging oaths.

For the African Americans who remained in the United States, life was still uncertain. All of the 13 colonies had practiced slavery before the war. Many of the enslaved Africans who joined the British were left behind and forced back into bondage. Pennsylvania was the first state to pass a Gradual Abolition Act in 1780, which provided a way for many enslaved Africans to obtain freedom. By 1790, there were about 2,000 free Africans living in Philadelphia. The New England states followed soon after, with New York passing a Gradual Abolition Act in 1799. The southern states would remain economically dependent on enslaved labor until the Civil War.

The war also had a profound impact on Native Americans. The 1784 Treaty of Fort Stanwix imposed peace on the members of the Iroquois Confederacy that sided with the British—but even those who sided with the Americans were soon under increasing pressure as settlers moved farther west.

THE U.S. CONSTITUTION OF 1787

Although the Articles of Confederation had bound the states together during the war, its weaknesses soon became apparent. The central government had authority over foreign affairs, but little else. It had no power to levy taxes, control trade between the states, or even mint money.

Congress Hall: The large building on the corner was constructed as a courthouse but used by the U.S. Congress from 1790 to 1800.

In May 1787, delegates from 12 states (Rhode Island did not attend) met at the Pennsylvania State House in Philadelphia to revise the Articles of Confederation. This Constitutional Convention was held in the same chamber where the Declaration was adopted. The delegates selected George Washington to preside over the convention, knowing that his presence would lend authority to the group. Then they established that each state would have one vote and that a majority would rule. To facilitate the free exchange of ideas and compromises, all discussions and actions were to be kept secret during the convention.

At the start, Edmund Randolph presented the Virginia Plan, which called for a new frame of government rather than modifying the Articles of Confederation. Under this plan, the government would have three branches: a legislative branch with a Congress to make laws; an executive branch with a president to execute the laws; and a judicial branch with a court system to enforce laws. James Madison authored this new plan. After serious debate, the delegates agreed to the Virginia Plan as a starting point. Then they set to work, ironing out the details.

CONFLICT IN THE CONSTITUTION

One major issue was balancing the interests of the large states and the small states. Under the Articles, each state had one vote—a system that favored small states such as Delaware. Large states like Virginia argued for representation based upon population. In mid-July, Roger Sherman of Connecticut presented a solution. Under the Connecticut Compromise, the legislative branch would have two houses. Each state would have an equal number in the Senate. In the House of Representatives, the number would be based upon the state's population. Later, they agreed that enslaved Africans would count as three-fifths of a person but not have the right to vote.

Another contentious issue was the slave trade. By 1787, six of the northern states had either abolished slavery or begun the gradual abolition of slavery. The southern states, however, were adamant that enslaved labor was vital to their economic survival. Concerned that the issue of slavery would prevent the ratification of the Constitution, the delegates chose to postpone the debate by agreeing that Congress could not make any laws regarding the importation of slaves until 1808. This decision caused division in the nation until all enslaved people were freed by the 13th Amendment to the Constitution in 1865.

> *"I have often and often in the course of Session, and the vicissitudes of my hopes and fears as to its issue, looked at that [sun] behind the President without being able to tell whether it was rising or setting. But now at length I have the happiness to know that it is a rising and not a setting Sun."*
>
> — Benjamin Franklin, after the signing of the Constitution of the United States, 1787

The delegates also argued over whether the president should be elected directly by the people or by the legislature. Finally, they decided that electors chosen from each state would vote for presidential candidates. The man with the most votes would become president for a term of four years, and the man with the second highest number of votes would become vice president. On September 17, 1787, the delegates signed the final draft of the Constitution and sent it to the states for ratification.

THE FIGHT OVER RATIFICATION

Delaware was the first state to ratify the Constitution, on December 7, 1787, earning the right to be called "The First State." Pennsylvania ratified soon after. But some states debated for months, polarizing the new nation.

We the People: The U.S. Constitution, only four pages long, has lasted over 200 years with amendments. It has become the model for constitutions all over the world.

John Jay: John Jay of New York helped write the *Federalist Papers*, which urged ratification. Appointed the first chief justice of the Supreme Court, he later negotiated the 1795 treaty with Great Britain. "Jay's Treaty" was widely unpopular, but it restored trade and removed British troops from America's Northwest Territories.

On one side were Federalists (who supported a strong central government), and on the other were Anti-Federalists (who preferred stronger state governments). In the Federalist camp were Alexander Hamilton, James Madison, and John Jay, who wrote the *Federalist Papers*, a persuasive series of newspaper articles that urged ratification. Patrick Henry and George Mason of Virginia were among the Anti-Federalists. They argued strongly against ratification, concerned that there was nothing in the Constitution that protected individual rights. Finally, both camps agreed to add amendments to the Constitution to protect individual liberties. Nine months after the signing of the Constitution, on June 21, 1788, New Hampshire became the ninth state to ratify the Constitution. Philadelphia held a grand parade to celebrate the occasion.

Road to Inauguration: This print shows Washington passing through the bridge at Trenton, New Jersey, on his way to be inaugurated as first president of the United States.

Once the Constitution was approved, Congress held the first national election. The electoral college unanimously voted for George Washington as the first president of the United States; John Adams, who received the second most votes, became vice president. On April 30, 1789, George Washington took the oath of office while standing on the balcony of Federal Hall in New York City. Then he gave his first inaugural address to Congress in the Senate chamber of Federal Hall.

BILL OF RIGHTS

At the same time that Washington and Adams took office, the first Congress opened session in New York, starting work on amendments to the Constitution that would guarantee individual rights. James Madison, a member of the House of Representatives, introduced the 10 amendments—now called the Bill of Rights. After many modifications, the amendments were sent to the states and ratified in 1791, after the federal government had moved to Philadelphia.

James Madison:
James Madison introduced the first amendments to the Constitution. Twelve amendments were proposed to Congress, but only 10 were ratified to become the Bill of Rights.

George Washington's Inauguration: Since no Supreme Court justices had yet been appointed, Robert Livingston, the chancellor of New York (seated, on Washington's left), administered the oath of office to Washington.

The Bill of Rights became both a symbol and the foundation of the American ideals of individual liberty, such as freedom of religion, freedom of the press, freedom of speech, the rule of law, and limited government. In effect, these measures made the Constitution not only an instrument of governmental power, but also a defender of liberty.

★ 73

CAPITAL OF THE UNITED STATES

Philadelphia's key role in early American history did not end with the signing of the Constitution. From 1790 to 1800, the city served as the temporary capital of the United States while the federal city was being built in Washington, D.C.

> *"The flames kindled on the Fourth of July, 1776, have spread over too much of the globe to be extinguished by the feeble engines of despotism; on the contrary, they will consume these engines and all who work them."*
>
> — Thomas Jefferson, in a letter to John Adams, September 12, 1821

During those ten years, all three branches of government worked within one block of each other. Congress met on the west side of the State House in a building now called Congress Hall. The House of Representatives sat on the first floor; the Senate met upstairs. The U.S. Supreme Court held sessions on the east side of the same block in City Hall beginning in 1791. A mansion one block north at 6th and Market streets served as the President's House and the seat of the executive branch of the federal government. George Washington lived and governed there for almost seven years, and John Adams occupied the home for three years.

During the 10 years the government was in Philadelphia, many important things were accomplished. Three new states were admitted to the Union, and the country's finances were improved by creating a new currency, a Bank of the United States, and the first Mint. The Jay Treaty with Great Britain was also debated and ratified by the Senate. One of the new country's most important events took place in March 1797 in Congress Hall: the first peaceful transfer of executive power. There, John Adams took his oath of office as the nation's second president. George Washington had decided not to run again and had given up the office, and Thomas Jefferson had peacefully conceded the election to Adams. All three men were present in Congress Hall that day with many others to witness the Republic's successful change of executives.

A HISTORIC LEGACY

In the summer of 1800, the federal government moved to Washington, D.C., and Philadelphia ceased to be the nation's capital. Yet the city continued to play a major role in American life.

In the 19th century, Philadelphia was a center of banking and finance, and with the development of manufacturing plants, foundries, railroads, and canals, it grew to be a major industrial city. Before the Civil War, the city was a major stop on the Underground Railroad, with Philadelphia's sizable free black population helping those seeking freedom from slavery. The 1876 Centennial Exposition, which celebrated the nation's 100th anniversary, brought more than nine million people to Fairmount Park. Meanwhile, the legacy left by Benjamin Franklin and other founders helped Philadelphia to develop into a center of science, education, culture, and religious tolerance.

1876 Centennial Exposition Poster: Millions thronged to Philadelphia in the summer of 1876 to see the World's Fair, which for the first time included a women's pavilion.

Today, the principles set forth by William Penn and the Founding Fathers can be felt everywhere in the city. From the Historic Square Mile, where a new nation was created, to the Parkway Museum District, the city's spirit of innovation, culture, and history lives on.

Early American Historic Sites

In 1751, the Pennsylvania Assembly ordered a 2,000-pound bell from London to hang in the new bell tower of the State House—now called Independence Hall. It was the 50th anniversary of William Penn's 1701 Charter of Privileges, Pennsylvania's original constitution, which granted religious freedom and political self-government to the colony. Isaac Norris, the Assembly speaker, requested that a Bible verse be placed on the bell: "Proclaim liberty throughout all the land unto all the inhabitants thereof" (Leviticus 25:10).

Liberty Bonds: The Liberty Bell was used as an effective symbol to raise funds during World War I.

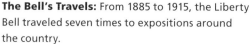

The Bell's Travels: From 1885 to 1915, the Liberty Bell traveled seven times to expositions around the country.

The new bell arrived in Philadelphia in 1752. Soon after, it cracked and was recast by two Philadelphia metal workers, John Pass and John Stow, who put their names and the date on the front of the bell. As the official bell of the State House, it rang to call legislators to the Assembly and for the opening of court sessions. It also rang in 1766 to celebrate the repeal of the unpopular Stamp Act.

Before the British occupied Philadelphia in 1777, the State House Bell and the bells from Christ Church were hastily moved to prevent them falling into British hands and being made into cannon. The State House Bell remained hidden under the floor of the Zion Reformed Church in Allentown until the British left Philadelphia in June 1778.

Symbol of Freedom: The City of Philadelphia purchased the old State House (Independence Hall) with its bell from the state in 1818. Today, the Liberty Bell is an internationally recognized symbol of freedom that attracts people from all over the world.

In 1781, the decaying steeple was removed, and the bell was lowered into the brick part of the tower. Still, the bell continued to ring, calling the state legislature into session, summoning voters to hand in their ballots at the State House window, and celebrating the Fourth of July. By 1846, a thin crack began to affect the sound. The bell was repaired by widening the hairline crack to prevent its sides from rubbing together. That year, when it rang to commemorate George Washington's birthday, the crack grew. The bell has not been rung since.

Its ring silenced, the bell began a new role as a symbol of liberty. The *Anti-Slavery Record* noted the Bible verse on the bell and referred to it as the Liberty Bell in its February 1835 issue. Other abolition groups used drawings of the Liberty Bell in their literature. In 1847, George Lippard wrote a popular tale in the *Philadelphia Saturday Courier* that invented a Revolutionary War connection. In the story, an old bell ringer waits in the State House tower on July 4, 1776. As he begins to doubt whether the Continental Congress will declare independence,

Recasting the Bell: The Liberty Bell was recast soon after it arrived in 1752. It weighs 2,080 pounds and is an alloy of copper and tin with small amounts of gold, silver, lead, zinc, and arsenic.

his grandson, who is eavesdropping on the deliberations, suddenly yells, "Ring, Grandfather! Ring!" This fictional story soon became popular.

> *"The old Independence Bell rang its last clear note on Monday last in honor of the birthday of Washington and now hangs in the great city steeple irreparably cracked and dumb."*
>
> — *Philadelphia Public Ledger*, February 26, 1846

Surveying the Crack: Before the Liberty Bell was moved out of Independence Hall in 1976, the National Park Service X-rayed it to ensure the crack had not expanded.

The Bell's Inscription: The top line on the bell is from the Bible: "Proclaim liberty throughout all the land . . ." (Leviticus 25:10). The second line, which indicates that the bell was ordered by the "Assembly of the Province of Pensylvania," uses an early spelling for the state.

In 1852, the Liberty Bell was moved down into the first-floor Assembly Room for easier viewing. After the Civil War, it also became a symbol of unity, reminding Americans of when they fought together for independence during the Revolutionary War. Beginning in the 1880s, the Liberty Bell traveled to various cities and expositions in the United States. However, there was growing worry that the crack might spread, so the trips ended. The bell returned to its home in Philadelphia in 1915. That same year, suffragists made a copy of the bell—calling it the Justice Bell—to use in their successful campaign to secure the right of women to vote.

Today, the Liberty Bell is displayed in the Liberty Bell Center on 6th Street as part of Independence National Historical Park. Here, exhibits tell its continuing history, such as its use by the civil rights movement and others seeking liberty. Standing in front of large windows that look out on Independence Hall, it can be viewed day and night.

The Liberty Bell: The Liberty Bell Center was designed to allow visitors to view the Liberty Bell with Independence Hall, its original home, in the background.

For ten years, an elegant three-story brick house on Market Street served as the nation's Executive Mansion, or White House. George Washington used the home from 1790 to 1797, and John Adams resided there from 1797 to 1800. At the President's House, they lived with their families, entertained, and governed the country.

Washington met with his cabinet and signed laws in the upstairs offices. He approved a national banking system, which stabilized the country's finances, and held firm to a foreign policy of neutrality in the war between France and England. Treasury Secretary Alexander Hamilton supported this policy, however, Secretary of State Thomas Jefferson did not, leaving the cabinet in protest. Despite Washington's attempts at consensus, political parties developed to reflect differing political goals.

"It is, I believe, the best single house in the city."

— George Washington, in a letter describing the President's House, circa 1790

Thirty people lived in the President's House with Washington, including two of Martha's grandchildren, Nelly and Wash. Washington's secretary, Tobias Lear, and his family resided there, as did many servants, who helped the Washingtons hold weekly receptions and dinners.

The President's House stood one block from Independence Hall, where the words "All men are created equal" were adopted but did not apply to everyone. Like many government officials, Washington owned enslaved servants, including nine enslaved Africans he brought to the President's House from Mount Vernon.

★ ★ PHILADELPHIA FIRSTS ★ ★

Many firsts occurred at the President's House Site, such as the first cabinet meeting, called by Washington in 1791.

Pennsylvania's 1780 gradual abolition law stated that enslaved Africans would be freed after six months of continuous residence in the state.

600 Market Street, Philadelphia, PA 19106 • (800) 537-7676

To prevent his slaves from claiming their freedom, Washington arranged to rotate them out of state every few months. He also signed the Fugitive Slave Act in 1793, which made it a federal crime to aid a slave's escape and denied them legal defense or a trial by jury. Despite this law, Philadelphia's free black population continued to grow and actively supported the antislavery movement. One of Martha Washington's enslaved servants, Oney Judge, escaped to freedom from the President's House in 1796.

In contrast to Washington, John Adams and his wife, Abigail, had simple tastes and entertained much less often. Abigail had an aversion to slavery and used only a few paid servants to run the household.

House Remains: At the President's House Site, archeologists were able to uncover part of the basement walls and the foundation for the bow window in the parlor.

After Adams left in 1800 for the nation's new capital in Washington, D.C., the President's House became a hotel and then a boardinghouse. It was torn down in 1832. Now a commemorative open-air exhibit tells the story of the President's House and its inhabitants. Opened in 2010 as part of Independence National Historical Park, the exhibit honors the enslaved African Americans who lived and toiled there.

The President's House Site: Opened in 2010, this open-air commemoration pays homage to the documented enslaved Africans who lived and worked at the house during Washington's presidency. The layout allows visitors to walk through the first floor as it appeared in the 18th century.

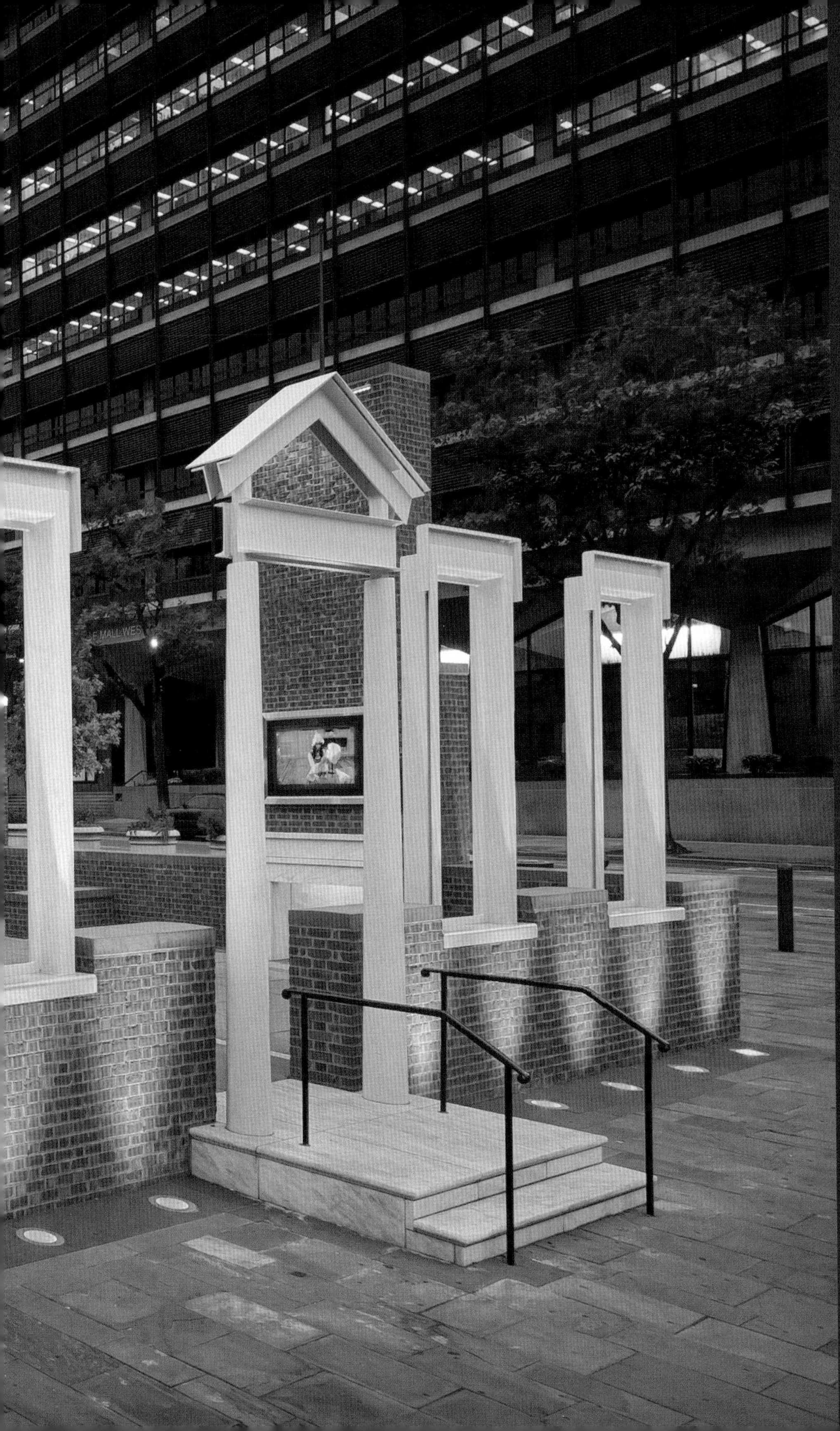

George Washington was born in Virginia in 1732 to a prosperous plantation owner. When he was 11, Washington's father died, and his half-brother Lawrence took him under his wing. As a teen, Washington became a land surveyor, which gave him a solid grounding in mathematics and topography. These subjects later served him well as a military commander.

Washington was a lieutenant colonel in the Virginia militia during the French and Indian War in 1754, commanding troops in the Battle of Fort Necessity. He married a wealthy widow, Martha Dandridge Custis, in January 1759. The couple had no children of their own but raised Martha's together. In 1761, he inherited Mount Vernon, a plantation on the Potomac River. Washington spent the next 15 years as a planter and a representative in Virginia's colonial legislature.

Washington at the Battle of Trenton: More than six feet tall, General Washington looked imposing when leading his troops on horseback. The Battle of Trenton took place on December 26, 1776, after Washington and his army crossed the Delaware River.

George Washington was elected to the Second Continental Congress in 1775, where he was commissioned commander in chief of the Continental Army. He took command on July 3. For the colonies' ill-trained troops, Washington's leadership in keeping them together early in the war was critical. One of his successful moves was leading his troops over the icy Delaware River on Christmas night in 1776, capturing Trenton and then Princeton, New Jersey. This three-week campaign restored the soldiers' morale and helped the cause of the American Revolution.

> *"Our Washington is no more. The hero, the patriot, and the sage of America; the man on whom in times of danger every eye was turned, and all hopes were placed, lives now only in his own great actions, and in the hearts of an affectionate and afflicted people."*
>
> — John Marshall, a member of the House of Representatives, confirming George Washington's death

After the British surrendered at Yorktown in 1781 and the peace treaty was signed in 1783, Washington resigned his military commission and retired to Mount Vernon. He was elected to the Constitutional Convention in 1787 and served as its presiding officer. Elected unanimously as the nation's first president, Washington served two terms—from 1789 to 1797. He could have served a third; instead, he established the precedent of a two-term maximum, which remained unchallenged until 1940.

Washington returned to his beloved Mount Vernon in 1797 at age 65. He had only a few years to enjoy his retirement. In December 1799, after he spent a day riding in foul weather, his throat became inflamed. He died the next day from a severe infection. A lifelong slaveholder, Washington freed his bondspeople in his will, which took effect after his wife died. The nation mourned his death for months.

At Independence Hall: This sculpture of George Washington by Joseph Bailly was placed in front of Independence Hall in 1910.

The Pennsylvania State House, known today as Independence Hall, is the birthplace of the United States of America. It was in the Assembly Room of this building that the Second Continental Congress debated and signed the Declaration of Independence in 1776. Eleven years later, in 1787, delegates to the Constitutional Convention met in the building to discuss, draft, and sign the Constitution of the United States.

Revolutionary Headquarters: For most of the Revolutionary War, the Continental Congress governed the country from Independence Hall, then called the Pennsylvania State House.

Construction began on the Pennsylvania State House in 1732. Master carpenter Edmund Wooley supervised the work based upon noted Philadelphia lawyer Andrew Hamilton's design. The State Assembly (legislature) moved into the building in September 1735 while construction was still under way.

The Pennsylvania State House was an ambitious public building for a colony. Its first floor included rooms for the state supreme court and the legislative assembly, while the second floor housed the governor's council chamber, a committee room, and a grand gallery for banquets and entertainment. There were wing buildings on each side and an impressive bell tower, added in 1750.

520 Chestnut Street, Philadelphia, PA 19106 • (800) 537-7676

In May 1775, delegates to the Second Continental Congress met in the State House Assembly Room to discuss concerns over England's restrictive policies. There, over the course of 12 years, representatives would write the new nation's legislative framework: the Declaration of Independence in 1776, the Articles of Confederation in 1777, and the Constitution of the United States in 1787.

Declaration of Independence: George Washington's portrait was added to this version of the Declaration of Independence even though he was not one of the signers. Washington was in New York, leading the Continental Army.

Independence Hall: This hand-colored engraving of Independence Hall features the signers of the Declaration of Independence with patriotic symbols around the border.

After 1800, both the national and state capitals left Philadelphia, and the State House was put to new uses. The City of Philadelphia bought the building—along with the old State House Bell (later called the Liberty Bell)—from the state for municipal purposes. Artist Charles Willson Peale displayed portraits of Revolutionary War heroes and his natural history collection in a museum on the second floor. In 1824, the Assembly Room found new life as the city prepared to host the Marquis de Lafayette during a stop on his American tour. General Lafayette was a French officer and close friend of General Washington's, and served under him during the Revolutionary War. City officials decided to refurbish the room in preparation for an elaborate ceremony to be held there. It was during this period that the Assembly Room was first called the "Hall of Independence," and the State House yard was named Independence Square.

Independence Hall: William Strickland designed the building's beautiful wooden bell tower in 1828 as an early example of restoration architecture. The original colonial tower did not have clock faces on its sides.

In the years that followed, the Assembly Room was seen increasingly as a historic shrine while the building continued to be used for municipal courts and offices. In 1854, the first floor was opened as a museum dedicated to the Revolutionary period; the second floor held high profile fugitive slave trials from 1850 to 1853. The irony of liberty proclaimed and denied in the same building was not lost on the antislavery crowds keeping watch in Independence Square during these hearings.

As a symbol of the founding of America, Independence Hall and Square became a favorite location for speeches. Three noted speakers were fugitive slave and author Frederick Douglass in 1844, President–elect Abraham Lincoln in 1861, and women's rights advocate Susan B. Anthony in 1876.

> *"I am filled with deep emotion at finding myself standing here in the place where were collected together the wisdom, the patriotism, the devotion to principle, from which sprang the institutions under which we live."*
>
> — Abraham Lincoln, speaking in Independence Hall, February 22, 1861

In 1828, the city replaced the wooden steeple on the bell tower with one designed by architect William Strickland. A new bell was hung in the tower for the centennial in 1876. As more and more people visited the building, local citizens established the Independence Hall Association in 1942. Their efforts led Congress to create Independence National Historical Park on June 28, 1948. Independence Hall was restored for the country's bicentennial in 1976 and designated a World Heritage site by the United Nations in 1979. Today, the West Wing of the hall includes surviving copies of the Declaration of Independence, the Articles of Confederation, and the Constitution of the United States in its Great Essentials exhibit. More than 600,000 people visit Independence Hall each year.

★ ★ **PHILADELPHIA FIRSTS** ★ ★

Congress Hall was the site of the first peaceful transfer of executive power when John Adams was inaugurated there in 1797 as the nation's second president. Washington declined a third term, and Thomas Jefferson conceded the election to Adams.

Philadelphia served as the temporary capital of the United States from 1790 to 1800 while the city of Washington, D.C., was being built. During this time, the House of Representatives and Senate met at Congress Hall, a two-story brick building to the west of the State House (now Independence Hall).

The House of Representatives met on the ground floor, while the Senate assembled upstairs. Several members of Congress who served there would later become president of the United States, including James Madison, James Monroe, Andrew Jackson, and William Henry Harrison. John Adams presided over the Senate as the country's first vice president.

It was in Congress Hall that three new states were admitted into the Union: Vermont, Kentucky, and Tennessee. Congress also created the U.S. Mint and the national currency system, debated treaties, and established the Department of the Navy and the First Bank of the United States. One of the most significant events was

Congress Hall: This brick building on the west side of Independence Hall is almost identical to Old City Hall on the east side except for the addition of a balcony.

when John Adams was inaugurated as the nation's second president in the House chamber in 1797, marking the nation's first peaceful transfer of executive power. (George Washington had taken his oath for his second term as president in the Senate chamber four years earlier.)

In 1800, the federal government relocated to Washington, and the building once again became the Philadelphia County Courthouse. Except for the enlargement of its south facade in 1793, the exterior has changed little. The building's interior was restored to its 1793 appearance by Independence National Historical Park.

House of Representatives Chamber: Located on the main floor of Congress Hall, this room was restored with reproduction furniture to match the original, including 18th-century style wall-to-wall carpeting. Here, George Washington witnessed John Adams being inaugurated as the nation's second president, with Thomas Jefferson as vice president.

Philadelphia's first City Hall was built during William Penn's lifetime on 2nd Street near the Delaware River. The second city hall—Old City Hall—sits on 5th Street to the east of Independence Hall. Completed in 1791, it was used by the U.S. Supreme Court until 1800, when the federal government moved to Washington, D.C. The Supreme Court held sessions on the first floor of the hall, sharing space with the mayor's court.

Many of the Supreme Court's early justices were signers of the Declaration of Independence and/or the Constitution, including Oliver Ellsworth, James Wilson, and John Blair. John Jay, one of the Supreme Court's most prominent justices, cowrote the *Federalist Papers* with Alexander Hamilton and James Madison, urging ratification of the U.S. Constitution. Jay served as chief justice from 1789 to 1795. He negotiated the controversial but important Jay Treaty in 1796 between England and the United States.

Old City Hall: This building housed the country's first U.S. Supreme Court from 1791 to 1800. Its large windows, minimal marble, and arched doorway reveal the Federal style of architecture that was popular after the American Revolution.

The second floor offices in Old City Hall also saw some historically significant events. During the grim three months of the 1793 yellow fever epidemic, the space served as volunteer headquarters. From his second floor office, Mayor Matthew Clarkson directed volunteers such as banker Stephen Girard and ministers such as Richard Allen and Absalom Jones of the Free African Society. Supplies like linens, food, and coffins were distributed, and the office was washed down daily with vinegar as a precaution. When the federal government left in 1800, the municipal government and courts occupied the building for almost 100 years. Today, Old City Hall is part of Independence National Historical Park.

The American Philosophical Society (APS) was founded in 1743 by Benjamin Franklin to "promote useful knowledge." It is the oldest learned society in the United States. Initially, the society met at various sites, including Carpenters' Hall. In 1789, the society moved into a new building—Philosophical Hall.

The APS was established as a home for its members to discuss nature, machines, industry, and governance. Its name is derived from the concept of "natural philosophy," the 18th century term for the study of nature. Since its inception, the society has had 15 signers of the Declaration of Independence, more than 200 Nobel Prize winners, and over a dozen presidents among its ranks. Members have included Thomas Jefferson, Albert Einstein, Charles Darwin, and Madame Curie.

Philosophical Hall: Owned by the American Philosophical Society, Philosophical Hall is the only private building on Independence Square. The society has promoted useful knowledge in the sciences and humanities for more than 250 years.

Philosophical Hall had various tenants over the years. The University of Pennsylvania held classes there, calling its students with the ringing of the nearby State House (Liberty) Bell. Artist Charles Willson Peale used the hall for his natural history museum before it moved to the State House. His museum featured plant and animal specimens, including the giant bones of an extinct mastodon.

Now a National Historic Landmark, the hall is open to the public as the Museum of the American Philosophical Society. Items in the collection include William Penn's original 1701 Charter of Privileges, which gave settlers the ability to establish their own laws; an armchair used by Thomas Jefferson while writing the Declaration of Independence; and Benjamin Franklin's clock and library chair. The museum also features artwork such as an original Gilbert Stuart portrait of George Washington, a portrait of Mrs. Benjamin (Deborah) Franklin, and Thomas Sully portraits of Thomas Jefferson and Dr. Benjamin Rush.

★ ★ **PHILADELPHIA FIRSTS** ★ ★

The American Philosophical Society, established by Benjamin Franklin in 1743, was the first scientific society in the country.

Benjamin Franklin: This sculpture by John Boyle sits on the main campus of Philadelphia's University of Pennsylvania, which Benjamin Franklin helped to found. Although he had just two years of formal schooling, Franklin valued education and never stopped learning.

Benjamin Franklin—one of the first great Americans—was a printer, statesman, inventor, diplomat, writer, scientist, entrepreneur, civic leader, and businessman. Born in Boston in 1706, he was the 15th child of a soap and candle maker. Franklin received some formal education but was mostly self-taught.

As a boy, he was apprenticed to his half-brother James, a printer who founded the *New England Courant*, the fourth newspaper in the colonies.

> *"What is serving God?*
> *Tis doing Good to Man."*
> — Benjamin Franklin,
> *Poor Richard's Almanack*, 1747

Franklin moved to Philadelphia in 1723, where six years later he published the *Pennsylvania Gazette*, turning it from a dull, poorly managed paper to the most successful newspaper in the colonies. His most profitable venture, however, was *Poor Richard's Almanack*. Published annually from 1732 to 1758, the *Almanack* included witty and wise sayings that preached frugality, industry, and thrift.

In 1728, Franklin fathered a son, William, with an unknown woman. Two years later, he entered into a common law marriage with his longtime friend and sweetheart, Deborah Read Rogers, whose husband had left her. The Franklins raised William and had a son and a daughter. Deborah managed the household and helped run a bookshop and a general store.

Working with a group of 12 friends who called themselves the Junto Society, Franklin sought to improve his city and the lives of his fellow Philadelphians. He formed the Library Company, the first subscription-circulating library in the nation in 1731; the Union Fire Company in 1736; the American Philosophical Society in 1743; and Pennsylvania Hospital in 1751. The following year, he cofounded the Philadelphia Contributionship for Insurance Against Loss by Fire. These are all still in existence today, with the Fire Company now a city agency. He also helped launch projects to pave, clean, and light Philadelphia's streets.

Franklin's career as a statesman began in 1736, when he served in the colonial legislature. He was named postmaster of Philadelphia in 1737, working his way up to become the deputy postmaster general of the colonies in 1753. In true Franklin fashion, he revamped the entire system to make it more reliable, inventing a device that could measure distances and thus improve mail routes.

In the early 1750s, he retired from printing and turned his focus to science. Franklin's famous experiments with electricity led him to coin the terms "negative," "positive," and "battery" and to invent the lightning rod. Other Franklin inventions included a heat-efficient stove, swim fins, bifocals, and an odometer.

> ★ ★ **PHILADELPHIA FIRSTS** ★ ★
>
> *In September 1752, Benjamin Franklin set up the world's first lightning rod at his home in Philadelphia, on the southeast corner of 2nd and Race streets.*

Franklin's Battery: This is the original battery Franklin created to store electricity for experiments. The glass jars, which held electrical charges, were linked by metal rods.

BENJAMIN FRANKLIN - CRAFTSMAN

Printer and Author: Franklin was a skilled writer and printer. Even when he was serving in France as the American ambassador, he set up a small press for his use.

Franklin's work expanded beyond the colonies in 1757, when he sailed to England as an agent for Pennsylvania and later Georgia, New Jersey, and Massachusetts. At first, as a loyal Englishman, he was surprised by the colonies' overwhelming opposition to the 1765 Stamp Act. But he eventually changed his position, and his testimony helped persuade Parliament to repeal the law.

Holding Court: Franklin traveled to France to serve as the American ambassador in December 1776. There, 70-year-old Franklin (pictured at center) charmed the French court, including 23-year-old King Louis XVI (seated with 20-year-old Queen Marie Antoinette).

In May 1775, Franklin gave up trying to change the policies of the king and Parliament and returned to Philadelphia. He was appointed to the Continental Congress and served on the committee to draft the Declaration of Independence in the summer of 1776. Five months later, he set sail again for Europe—bringing two of his grandsons along with him—and began a career as a diplomat. Franklin's scientific reputation made him a well-known figure abroad. He charmed the French court, helping to secure the alliance with France during the Revolutionary War. Afterward, Franklin, John Adams, and John Jay negotiated the Treaty of Paris, which ended the War for Independence in 1783.

In 1785, Franklin returned to Philadelphia, where he remodeled his properties and served as president (governor) of Pennsylvania and president of the Pennsylvania Society for the Abolition of Slavery. Franklin, the oldest member of the Constitutional Convention, urged all the delegates to sign the new Constitution on September 17, 1787. Although Franklin had owned slaves himself, his final public act was supporting a petition against slavery. On April 17, 1790, at the age of 84, Benjamin Franklin passed away in Philadelphia. Thousands followed his coffin as he was laid to rest in Christ Church Burial Ground.

Library Hall: Built in 1959, this building reproduced architect William Thornton's original Georgian design of Library Hall. Thornton also designed the U.S. Capitol building in Washington, D.C.

Benjamin Franklin: After the American Revolution, artists used symbols from the ancient Roman Republic and the Greek democracies, as depicted on this toga-wearing statue of Benjamin Franklin.

B. FRANKLIN

REPLICA OF THE STATUE BY LAZZARINI
PRESENTED TO THE LIBRARY COMPANY 1792
BY WILLIAM BINGHAM

Founded in 1731 by Benjamin Franklin and his friends, the Library Company of Philadelphia was the nation's first successful lending library. The company was also a forerunner of the Library of Congress. Politicians meeting in Philadelphia were invited to use the resources of the nearby Library Company.

Library Hall: Among the Library Company's members were 11 signers of the Declaration of Independence, including founder Benjamin Franklin.

In 1790, the company built Library Hall—across from Philosophical Hall on 5th Street—to serve as its headquarters. It stayed there until the 1880s, when it outgrew the space and moved. The building was demolished in 1884. The original design was reproduced on the site in 1959, and today the American Philosophical Society owns the building.

The American Philosophical Society owns more than seven million manuscripts and thousands of books, maps, and prints. Some of its most significant holdings include Franklin's books and papers, the original journals of the Lewis and Clark expedition, a copy of the Declaration of Independence in Jefferson's own handwriting, a first edition of Sir Isaac Newton's *Principia*, and a first edition of Charles Darwin's *Origin of Species*. Exhibits in the lobby are open to the public during the week; the rest of the building is open by appointment only.

> ★ **PHILADELPHIA FIRSTS** ★
>
> *The Library Company of Philadelphia, the first subscription-based library in America, was founded in 1731 by Benjamin Franklin and others.*

105 South 5th Street, Philadelphia, PA 19106 • (215) 440-3400

Designed by William Strickland and modeled after the Parthenon, the Second Bank of the United States is one of the country's finest examples of Greek revival architecture. The marble building was constructed between 1819 and 1824 to house the Second Bank of the United States. This bank played a role similar to the United States' current Federal Reserve System.

Nicholas Biddle: Bank president Nicholas Biddle graduated from college at age 15 and then helped edit the Lewis and Clark journals for publication.

Second Bank of the United States: The Second Bank and other nearby buildings are sometimes referred to as America's First Wall Street.

The Second Bank was given a 20 year charter in 1816, after the charter for the First Bank of the United States had expired and the country was struggling to repay loans secured to finance the War of 1812. Under the leadership of bank president Nicholas Biddle, the bank became one of the most influential financial institutions in the world. It regulated the national economy, marketed government bonds, and provided credit for businesses. In 1832, the Second Bank became the center of a bitter controversy between Biddle and President Andrew Jackson over the bank's role in the national economy. Jackson vetoed the bill to extend the bank's charter, and in 1836, it ceased to exist. Afterward, the building was used as the United States Customs House for the port of Philadelphia. The building was designated a National Historic Site in June 1939, and in 1948, it became part of Independence National Historical Park.

Today, this elegant building houses the People of Independence exhibit, which features 185 paintings of early leaders by such painters as Gilbert Stuart, Thomas Sully, Charles Willson Peale, and others. There are portraits painted from life of Martha and George Washington, Dolley and James Madison, and a redheaded Thomas Jefferson. Mohawk leader Joseph Brant (Thayendanegea) also sat for a portrait on a diplomatic visit to Philadelphia in 1797. Many of the portraits painted by Peale were originally displayed in his museum on the second floor of Independence Hall.

420 Chestnut Street, Philadelphia, PA 19106 • (800) 537-7676

CHARLES WILLSON PEALE

Charles Willson Peale, an artist, naturalist, and soldier, was born on April 15, 1741, in Maryland. He was apprenticed to an Annapolis saddle maker, but he soon began to pursue painting. Peale was sent to London by wealthy patrons to study with American artist Benjamin West. He returned to Maryland, earning his living as a portrait painter before moving to Philadelphia in 1775.

Peale was an early supporter of American independence, fighting in the Philadelphia militia at the Battles of Trenton and Princeton from 1776 to 1777. But he made his real contribution as a painter—not a soldier. He painted portraits of notable patriots such as George Washington, John Paul Jones, John Adams, and Thomas Jefferson. Soon after the war, he began showing his art to the public in his home. He was the first to display animal specimens against realistic painted habitats. In 1786, he added natural history specimens of birds, mammals, and plants to his collection. Peale's museum was the first in America. It became so popular that he moved it to the American Philosophical Society at 5th and Chestnut streets. In 1802,

Charles Willson Peale: In this self-portrait, the artist lifts a curtain to reveal his museum to the public. People flocked to see Peale's portraits and animal specimens, which were usually only available to the rich.

the museum was relocated to the second floor of Independence Hall; today many of the portraits are on display in the Second Bank Portrait Gallery.

In 1805, Peale helped to found the oldest art school in America, the Pennsylvania Academy of the Fine Arts. Several of his children became professional artists. In addition, Moses Williams, his enslaved servant, earned his freedom and a good income by making popular silhouettes in Peale's museum. Peale continued to paint portraits until shortly before his death at age 85.

★ ★ **PHILADELPHIA FIRSTS** ★ ★

Charles Willson Peale established the Pennsylvania Academy of the Fine Arts, the first art school in America, in 1805.

Located in Independence National Historical Park, Carpenters' Hall is still owned and operated by the Carpenters' Company of the City and County of Philadelphia. The company, established in 1724, is the oldest trade guild in the United States. The Carpenters' Company completed the building in 1773 to showcase its members' skills. It also provided the organization with income from renting out space.

Carpenters' Hall: In the 18th century, Carpenters' Hall was located in a crowded, built-up neighborhood. The architects included spacious lawns around the building to help protect it from fire.

Carpenters' Hall was the site of many important "firsts." The Library Company of Philadelphia, the country's first subscription-based library, and the American Philosophical Society, the nation's first learned society, were located there. In 1774, it was the site of the First Continental Congress. Delegates from 12 colonies (except Georgia) arrived in Philadelphia on September 5 of that year, gathering at City Tavern. Joseph Galloway, the conservative speaker of the Pennsylvania Assembly, offered the State House as a meeting place, but the delegates chose Carpenters' Hall as a more neutral location. The First Continental Congress met for seven weeks. After much debate, they signed a Declaration of Colonial Rights, which was sent to King George.

Carpenters' Hall played an important role in December 1775 as the secret meeting place of Benjamin Franklin and French agent Julien-Alexandre Achard de Bonvouloir. Under the cover of darkness, they met in the room used by the Library Company. French support was vital for the Americans in their rebellion against England.

Following the Revolution, the building was rented to various tenants, such as the Bank of Pennsylvania. On September 2, 1798, Carpenters' Hall was the site of another first: the nation's first bank robbery. The thief, Isaac Davis, stole $162,821.61. The money was recovered when Davis began depositing his new wealth in the same bank! In 1857, the company repaired and opened the building as a historic shrine. It was one of the first private organizations to be open to the public.

320 Chestnut Street, Philadelphia, PA 19106 • (215) 925-0167

Located two blocks from Independence Square on Walnut Street are two historically important row homes: the Bishop White House and the Todd House.

From 1791 to 1793, lawyer John Todd, his wife, Dolley Payne Todd, and their family occupied the Todd House on 4th Street. Built in 1775, the house reflects the tastes and income of a young middle-class Quaker family. John Todd conducted his law practice in a room on the first floor. His clerk, Isaac Heston, lived with the family. During the 1793 yellow fever epidemic, Todd and Heston stayed in the city to take care of legal needs and died of the fever. Dolley, their son, Payne, and their newborn were sent to safety in the country. Sadly, the Todds' newborn son died, and Dolley returned to the city a widow. Her fortunes improved some months later when she was introduced to Congressman James Madison, who would become the fourth president of the United States. They had a long and happy marriage.

Near 3rd Street, Bishop William White and his wife, Mary, built a large elegant house in 1787, the same year he was ordained as the first Episcopal bishop of Pennsylvania. He chose the site because it stood between his two parishes: Christ Church and St. Peter's. White was the chaplain to the Continental Congress and later, the U.S. Senate. Eminent members of society frequented his home. The bishop's sister Mary White Morris and her husband, Robert Morris, were guests, along with Dr. Benjamin Rush and Francis Hopkinson. George Washington dined there as a private citizen on November 19, 1798. Bishop White lived in the home until his death in 1836. The restored home contains elegant furnishings, including many owned by White, and even an indoor "necessary," or privy—a luxury given that most privies were outside in the back garden at the time.

Bishop White House: William White brought large glass windowpanes from London and had to pay extra on his fire insurance to cover them.

The Todd House and the Bishop White House on Walnut Street are open by appointment only. The tour includes both sites. Tickets are available for free at the Independence Visitor Center.

Dolley Payne Todd Madison was born to John and Mary Coles Payne in Piedmont, North Carolina, in 1768. In 1783, her family moved to Philadelphia, where she grew up in the strict discipline of the Quaker faith. Dolley married John Todd Jr., a young lawyer, at a Quaker meetinghouse in 1790. The following year, they moved to a modest home on Walnut Street, where she gave birth to two sons. Dolley and John were married for just three years. In 1793, John succumbed to yellow fever. Their infant son passed away the same day.

Widowed at 27 with a young son, Dolley was considered warm, attractive, and gregarious. A few months after the death of her husband, she was introduced to James Madison, 17 years her senior. They were married after a brief courtship on September 15, 1794. Since Madison was an Episcopalian, Dolley left the Quaker faith.

> *"It is one of my sources of happiness never to desire a knowledge of other people's business."*
>
> — Dolley Madison

In 1801, Madison became secretary of state, and Dolley filled the role of first lady for the widowed President Thomas Jefferson. Her warm personality and lavish parties at the White House dazzled the capital for years while her husband was president from 1809 to 1817. During the War of 1812, Dolley's reputation soared as she stayed at the White House until the last minute before fleeing the British troops. The large portrait of George Washington was also hastily removed and carried to safety. Dolley returned to find that the British had burned the building down, leaving it in ruins.

After the presidency, Dolley and James Madison retired to their plantation, Montpelier, in Virginia. Madison passed away in 1836, and the following year, Dolley returned to Washington, where she died in 1849.

The Right Reverend William White, one of Philadelphia's most famous and beloved residents, was a prominent Episcopalian bishop, chaplain, and community leader. Born in Philadelphia in 1748, White studied at the University of Pennsylvania and was ordained in England in 1772. He returned to Philadelphia the following year and married Mary Harrison, the daughter of a former Philadelphia mayor.

White was the rector of Christ Church and St. Peter's Church for 57 years. He served as chaplain of the Continental Congress for many years and later as chaplain for the U.S. Senate. During the Revolutionary War, he was one of the few Anglican clergymen who supported the Patriot cause, a decision that cost him money but made him popular with the citizens. After the war, he led the effort to create the American Episcopal Church, becoming one of the first consecrated bishops and the first Episcopal bishop of Pennsylvania.

Bishop White: William White was the first consecrated bishop of the Protestant Episcopal Church in Pennsylvania and chaplain of the Continental Congress and the U.S. Senate.

Christ Church Pulpit: Before microphones, ministers needed to be located up high to project their voices to the congregation.

Although White was not an inspiring preacher, he was a good theologian and an effective organizer. He founded the Episcopal Academy, the Pennsylvania School for the Deaf, and the Magdalen Society (known today as Philadelphia Futures)—education-based schools and organizations that are still active today. He also created organizations to educate African Americans and Native American students, and was involved in prison reform and missionary work. George Washington was a confidant of White's, giving money to White's charities. In the 1790s, the bishop stayed in Philadelphia during the yellow fever epidemics while many other men of wealth abandoned the city. After a long life of service, Reverend White died in his home at age 88 on July 17, 1836.

The Merchants' Exchange Building was built in 1834 to serve as Philadelphia's financial center. Previously, the city's merchants had met in coffeehouses or taverns near the docks, such as the London Coffee House and City Tavern. In 1831, a group of business leaders decided they needed a central location to carry out their business. Headed by Stephen Girard, the wealthiest man in the nation, the group selected William Strickland to design the building.

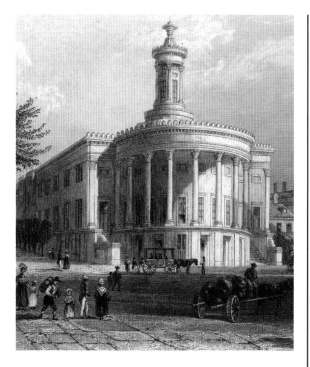

Merchants' Exchange Building: This 1839 engraving by William Henry Bartlett shows the Dock Street entrance to the Merchants' Exchange Building, home of the Philadelphia Stock Exchange.

Strickland was the architect of the acclaimed Second Bank of the United States. For the Merchants' Exchange, he devised a creative solution for the pointed plot of land along Dock Street, choosing to round the east end of the building. Once completed, the Merchants' Exchange housed commercial businesses on the ground floor; on the upper floors were various marine insurance companies, the Philadelphia Board of Trade, and the Philadelphia Stock Exchange. A U.S. Post Office on the Dock Street side of the ground floor was the first in the country to sell stamps.

The Merchants' Exchange Building was not the hub of economic activity for long. By the Civil War, just 30 years later, businesses had begun to move west. Broad Street became Philadelphia's new financial center, and the Merchants' Exchange Building began to deteriorate. In 1952, the National Park Service acquired the building and started to restore the structure. The building was designated a National Historic Landmark in 2001. Today, it serves as the headquarters of Independence National Historical Park. The first floor features an exhibit about the building that is open to the public during the week.

143 South 3rd Street, Philadelphia, PA 19106 • (215) 597-8787

One of Philadelphia's most influential citizens arrived in the city as a 26-year-old immigrant. Born in Bordeaux, France, in 1750, Stephen Girard spent his early life as a sea captain and merchant, trading goods between the American colonies and the West Indies. He came to Pennsylvania in June 1776, when a British blockade diverted him from New York. As a Frenchman, Girard had no great love for the British and decided to use his experience as a merchant to aid the Patriots. He officially became an American citizen on October 27, 1778.

Girard's reputation as a humanitarian began during the city's 1793 yellow fever epidemic. Girard stayed in Philadelphia and volunteered to take charge of the yellow fever hospital established outside the city. He brought in a French doctor who had experience with the disease, hired more competent staff, and personally supervised the hospital. After the crisis passed, he was recognized as a hero in a meeting held in City Hall.

"My deeds must be my life."
— Stephen Girard

Girard also became involved in politics. He lobbied the Washington administration to relax its policies on shipping; spoke out against the controversial Jay Treaty; campaigned for Thomas Jefferson in 1800; and advocated for a national bank. When the First Bank of the United States was established in 1791, Girard invested heavily. In 1811, the bank's charter expired, and Girard bought the bank and its assets, including the building, becoming the nation's most powerful banker virtually overnight.

His stature grew further when the U.S. Treasury ran out of money during the War of 1812. Without demanding concessions, Girard granted an eight million dollar loan to the Treasury, keeping the government from financial collapse and seeing the country through to the 1814 treaty with Britain. After the war ended, Girard supported the establishment of the Second Bank of the United States to help the nation regain its financial footing. He also led a group of prominent citizens in founding the city's Merchants' Exchange Building.

Girard died on December 26, 1831. In his will, he bequeathed money to many individuals and organizations, including several million dollars to build Girard College, a boarding school to educate underprivileged children. The school is still in operation today.

Merchants' Exchange Tower: Architect William Strickland needed to provide a tall tower to spot incoming ships, so he copied a popular drawing of an ancient Greek monument, the Choragic Monument of Lysicrates.

City Tavern, located at 2nd and Walnut streets, was a political, social, and business center of the early United States. Built in 1773 by the city's business leaders, the tavern was a gathering place for the wealthy citizens of Philadelphia, the colonies' largest and most cosmopolitan city. Inside the elegant three-story building, many of Philadelphia's business transactions took place. Colonists could have dinner, read the latest newspapers, conduct business deals, exchange promissory notes, enjoy a drink, hear a concert, and find a room for the night.

City Tavern Dining Room: In the 18th century, Philadelphia was known for its culinary excellence. Diners at City Tavern most likely enjoyed abundant fresh produce, seafood, and imported delicacies, such as pineapples from the West Indies.

The tavern's rich Revolutionary history began when delegates to the First Continental Congress arrived in Philadelphia the evening of September 4, 1774, and met in the tavern. Delegate John Adams called it "the most genteel tavern in America." Two weeks later, another famous Revolutionary figure reined up at the building: Paul Revere had brought a copy of the Boston-area declaration denouncing Parliament's Intolerable Acts—and had come to ask for Philadelphia's support. Revere returned to City Tavern seven months later, in April 1775, and announced that fighting had broken out at Lexington and Concord.

138 South 2nd Street, Philadelphia, PA 19106 • (215) 413-1443

Continental Congress: Delegates met at City Tavern before deciding on a location for the official meeting in the fall of 1774.

City Tavern: Tavern dining rooms served as places for informal political negotiations as well as formal banquets. Thomas Paine stayed at City Tavern when he first arrived in America.

When the Second Continental Congress convened in the city in May 1775, the tavern again became a favorite haunt of the delegates, including George Washington, Thomas Jefferson, and Ben Franklin. In 1787, City Tavern was the center of national politics when the city hosted the Constitutional Convention. After the members finished the final draft of the Constitution, they adjourned to the tavern to celebrate. One of the last notable events occurred in 1789, when George Washington celebrated with 250 Philadelphians prior to his inauguration in New York City.

City Tavern lost most of its business when the much larger Merchants' Exchange opened a block away in 1834. A fire damaged the tavern that same year, and the building was demolished in 1854. It was reconstructed in 1975 by the National Park Service and opened as a concession in Independence National Historical Park. Today, visitors to this 18th century tavern can enjoy a fine dining experience for a unique taste of history.

John Adams was one of America's most important Founding Fathers. Born in Massachusetts on October 30, 1735, he attended Harvard, taught school, and practiced law. In 1764, he married Abigail Smith, whom he called his "dear friend." They were married for 54 years and had four children, including John Quincy Adams, the sixth president of the United States.

> "Yesterday the greatest question was decided which ever was debated in America; and a greater perhaps never was, nor will be, decided among men. A resolution was passed without one dissenting colony, that these United Colonies are, and of right ought to be, free and independent States."
>
> — John Adams, in a letter to Abigail Adams, July 3, 1776

In 1761, John Adams began to write against those British measures that he believed infringed on colonial rights. Along with his cousin, Samuel Adams, he was an early supporter of independence from Britain. Adams was a delegate to the First and Second Continental Congresses in Philadelphia, serving on the committee to draft the Declaration of Independence. (He suggested that Thomas Jefferson write the Declaration.) In 1779, he drafted the Massachusetts Constitution, which became a model for the U.S. Constitution.

Adams also served as a diplomat. During the Revolutionary War, he traveled to France and Holland, securing loans and helping to negotiate the Treaty of Paris, which ended the war. Adams was the first American ambassador to Great Britain from 1785 to 1788. When George Washington became the first president in 1789, Adams was elected the first vice president.

John Adams was elected the second president of the United States in the first contested election, running against Thomas Jefferson and Aaron Burr. During his term (1797–1801), he kept many of Washington's policies, especially his neutrality in foreign affairs. When revolutionary France threatened American interests, Adams built up the armed forces, supported the establishment of a navy, and dispatched a peace commission to France. An independent-minded president, he often disagreed with his Federalist party (led by Alexander Hamilton) as well as Jefferson's new Democratic–Republican party.

John Adams: Adams was often away from his Massachusetts home and beloved wife, Abigail. Their letters to each other provide a valuable record of the early years of the country he did so much to establish.

Adam's Papers: John Adams was an intellectual who kept many journals and regularly corresponded with Thomas Jefferson, among others.

John and Abigail Adams retired to their beloved house in Quincy, Massachusetts, in 1801, after he lost the presidency to Thomas Jefferson. In 1812, at the urging of Benjamin Rush, Adams began corresponding with Jefferson. Their letters left a valuable legacy to the nation. Fittingly, both he and Jefferson died on the same day: July 4, 1826, the 50th anniversary of the adoption of the Declaration of Independence.

Benjamin Franklin's three-story, 10-room brick mansion once stood at the site of Franklin Court. Construction began on the house in 1763, and it was still being completed when Franklin traveled to England in 1765 to serve as a colonial agent for Pennsylvania. His wife, Deborah, and daughter Sally stayed behind. Letters between Ben and Deborah provide vivid details of the house's decor. Excerpts from these letters appear in the paving on the site of the original house.

Glass Armonica: This instrument, devised by Benjamin Franklin, has a series of glass bowls that rotate around a metal rod. By rubbing the edge of the glasses with wet fingertips, music "like that of the angels" could be played.

Franklin Court Ghost House: Steel beams outline the shape of Benjamin Franklin's house, located in the middle of his beloved City of Philadelphia.

Franklin lived in the house while serving in the Continental Congress from 1775 to 1776. He returned there in 1785 after living in France and stayed at the house until his death at 84 in 1790. Franklin's grandchildren inherited the house, but they found that no one wanted a large residential house in what had become a commercial district. The house was demolished in 1812 to make room for row houses. A road was built in the middle of the site, sealing the ruins of the basement kitchen and nearby privy. When the site was excavated beginning in the 1950s, pieces of the home's foundation were found, along with a rare Bristol punchbowl and other ceramics. Unfortunately, no historical records of the exterior exist.

316 Market Street, Philadelphia, PA 19106 • (800) 537-7676

> *"From a Child I was fond of Reading, and all the little Money that came into my Hands was ever laid out in Books."*
>
> — Benjamin Franklin, in his autobiography

Today, a steel "ghost structure" designed in 1976 by world-famous architect Robert Venturi outlines the shape of the house where it once stood. There are also portals that show the preserved foundation walls of Franklin's house. The Franklin Court complex, part of Independence National Historical Park, includes five brick row houses, three of which Franklin owned as rental properties.

★ ★ **PHILADELPHIA FIRSTS** ★ ★

Benjamin Franklin published the nation's first political cartoon in his Pennsylvania Gazette *newspaper on May 9, 1754, urging the colonies to "join or die" in dealing with their enemies.*

Visitors can see many artifacts in the Fragments of Franklin Court exhibit at 318 Market Street. Next door, a reproduction 18th century printing press is used to demonstrate the craft that made Franklin rich and famous. His grandson B. F. Bache's newspaper office, a major opposition paper

in the 1790s, is at 322 Market Street. Visitors can enter the Benjamin Franklin Museum, located under the courtyard, where displays, interactive exhibits, and original artifacts belonging to Franklin tell the story of this extraordinary American.

Join or Die: Franklin's powerful image of a cut up snake was based upon a popular 18th century belief that a snake would live if its parts were joined before sunset.

Founded in 1695, Christ Church was the first parish of the Anglican Church of England in Pennsylvania and the birthplace of the U.S. Episcopal Church. Christ Church Burial Ground is located at 5th and Arch streets, a few blocks from the church. The burial ground was established in 1719, when the original cemetery next to the church became full and the neighboring lands proved to be too marshy. Land for a new cemetery was purchased along 5th Street, which at the time was on the outskirts of town.

Dozens of colonial, Revolutionary, and early republic notables are interred at Christ Church Burial Ground. Benjamin Franklin, signer of the Declaration of Independence and the U.S. Constitution, and his wife, Deborah, are buried on the northwest corner. After Franklin's death in April 1790, a crowd of 20,000 mourners followed the procession to his grave. William Smith, provost of the University of Pennsylvania, gave the eulogy and the Comte de Mirabeau did the same before the French National Assembly in Paris.

Franklin's Grave: Located in a corner of the burial ground with a plain stone marker as he requested, Benjamin Franklin's grave is easy to locate. Several other Revolutionary-era printers are buried nearby.

Other famous Philadelphians buried at the site include Dr. Philip Syng Physick (1768–1837), father of American surgery, and Dr. Benjamin Rush (1745–1813), father of American psychiatry and a signer of the Declaration of Independence. Three other signers are buried there: George Ross, Joseph Hewes, and Francis Hopkinson. In addition, young children, sea captains, a safecracker, and many victims of the yellow fever epidemics of the 1790s are buried there. The burial ground is open to the public year-round except in winter.

20 N. American Street, Philadelphia, PA 19106 • (215) 922-1695

Christ Church: In recognition of the religious tolerance granted by William Penn in his Charter of Privileges, Independence National Historical Park has formal associations with historic churches of several denominations, including Christ Church.

When the call went out in 1776 for able-bodied men to bear arms in the colonial militia, a group of Quakers answered. These men—who numbered about 200—could not reconcile themselves to the Quaker principle of pacifism when it came to defending their country. Their decision to support the war effort was a painful one. They knew they would be disowned and "read out" of their meetings for failing to adhere to their Peace Testimony. For Quakers, fighting, selling, or making military supplies, taking a loyalty oath to the new American government, holding a position in a civil office, or paying war taxes could all result in expulsion from the faith.

> "True godliness doesn't turn men out of the world, but enables them to live better in it, and excites their endeavours to mend it."
>
> — William Penn, *No Cross No Crown*, written while he was imprisoned, 1682

Led by prominent Quaker merchant Samuel Wetherill, they formed the Religious Society of Free Quakers in 1781. They built their own place of worship, the Free Quaker Meeting House, on the southwest corner of 5th and Arch streets. Between 30 and 50 men and women regularly attended services there. Over the years, participation declined until just two members remained—Betsy Ross Claypoole and captain John Price Wetherill, son of Samuel Wetherill. In 1834, they discontinued their meetings for worship there.

The Free Quaker Meeting House: Following the Quaker tradition, this meeting house has no steeple outside and no altar inside. The interior only has benches facing each other.

The building was successively a school, an apprentice library, a plumbing warehouse, and a headquarters for the Junior League of Philadelphia. In 1957, the Free Quaker Meeting House was purchased by the state of Pennsylvania and restored to its 18th century appearance. It is now open to the public as part of Independence National Historical Park.

The Betsy Ross House reveals what a typical 18th century home was like in Philadelphia. Betsy ran her upholstery business from her home. Besides upholstering furniture, she learned to make curtains, venetian blinds, tents, and flags. In May 1777, she was paid to make flags for the Pennsylvania navy.

When the Continental Congress voted to adopt the U.S. flag on June 14, 1777, they needed flags with the 13 stars and 13 stripes. No one at the time recorded who made the first flag. But in 1870, as the nation prepared to celebrate the centennial of the Declaration of Independence, Betsy Ross's grandchildren began telling the story of how she was asked to sew the flag and had suggested the five-pointed star. This patriotic story caught the public's imagination. Soon, no visit to Philadelphia was complete without a visit to the "Betsy Ross Flag House."

Betsy Ross House: Betsy Ross, an upholsterer, is said to have lived in this house on Arch Street between 1773 and 1785.

The house at 239 Arch Street is open to the public with its seven rooms furnished in period furniture and some of Betsy's own possessions. There is a kitchen, parlor, bedrooms, and upholstery shop (though there is no bathroom). The complex includes exhibits, a garden, gift shop, and the graves of Betsy and her last husband.

Flag Maker: This 19th century painting depicts Betsy Ross cutting a five-pointed star. While the flag shows the stars in a circle, this design was not standardized until 1912.

Elizabeth "Betsy" Griscom Ross Ashburn Claypoole was born on January 1, 1752, to Samuel and Rebecca Griscom, who were members of the Religious Society of Friends, commonly called "Quakers." She grew up at 4th and Arch streets in Philadelphia as the eighth of 17 children.

After completing her formal education at a Quaker school, Betsy was apprenticed to a local upholsterer. There, she learned to make upholstered furniture, bedcovers, umbrellas, and military supplies such as uniforms, tents, and flags. She fell in love with another apprentice, John Ross. In 1773, they eloped and started their own upholstery business. Because her husband was an Anglican, not a Quaker, she was "read out" of the Quaker meeting and became an Anglican.

The war years were difficult for Betsy. In January 1776, John was wounded while serving in the local militia and soon died. She carried on the upholstery business, making items such as flags for the war effort. Betsy married sea captain Joseph Ashburn in 1777, but once again, tragedy struck: On a trip to the West Indies, Captain Ashburn was captured by the British and imprisoned in England. He died there five years later.

Her third husband was John Claypoole, an old friend who had been imprisoned with her late husband. They married in May 1783 and soon moved from

★ ★ **PHILADELPHIA FIRSTS** ★ ★

The first flag of the United States of America was sewn in Philadelphia in 1777.

Betsy's rented house on Arch Street to 2nd Street. A year later, Betsy returned to her Quaker roots when she and John joined the Society of Free Quakers, a group that actively supported the War for Independence. Betsy continued working in her upholstery business into her 70s with some of her daughters. She died on January 30, 1836, at the age of 84.

"Resolved: that the flag of the United States be made of thirteen stripes, alternate red and white; that the union be thirteen stars, white in a blue field, representing a new constellation."

— The Continental Congress, June 14, 1777

America's Oldest Residential Street: At Elfreth's Alley, visitors can see the kind of houses ordinary Philadelphians lived in during the 18th and 19th centuries. The homes there are still inhabited.

Elfreth's Alley, popularly known as the nation's "oldest residential street," is located off 2nd Street between Race and Arch streets near Christ Church. The alley was created around 1702. In 1750, it was named for Jeremiah Elfreth, who owned land on both sides of the alley.

Elfreth's Alley: Established in 1702, Elfreth's Alley was home to a diverse population of artisans and craftsmen in the 18th and early 19th centuries. Firemen, police officers, and clothing factory workers lived there in the early 20th century.

In the 18th century, this modest neighborhood of brick row houses was inhabited by a diverse group of carpenters, printers, seamen, and seamstresses. Benjamin Moses Mordecai, a Jewish merchant and leader of Mikveh Israel Synagogue, lived next door to English Anglican colonists who worshipped at Christ Church. Cophie Douglass, an African American, began his life as a free man in post-Revolutionary Philadelphia by living on Elfreth's Alley. Benjamin Franklin visited William Maugridge—a fellow member of the "Junto," a mutual self-improvement club—at number 122.

In the 19th century, the alley was home to recent immigrants from Germany and Ireland, many who worked nearby as firemen. In 1934, alley resident Dorothy Ottey organized a group of women and men to save several of the colonial houses from demolition. As one of the earliest historic preservation groups in Philadelphia, the Elfreth's Alley Association continues to carry out its mission of preservation and education. Today, all but the two museum houses are modern-day residential homes. The alley is a National Historic Landmark.

★ ★ **PHILADELPHIA FIRSTS** ★ ★

Philadelphia, established by William Penn in 1682, was the nation's first planned city, with straight streets, large lots, and five squares to prevent fires from spreading.

2nd Street (between Race and Arch), Philadelphia, PA 19106 • (215) 574-0560

POWEL HOUSE

Samuel Powel was the last colonial mayor of Philadelphia and the first mayor after the Revolution. He purchased this house—located in one of the most fashionable areas of 18th century Philadelphia—in 1769, when he married Elizabeth Willing. He furnished it with treasures acquired during his seven-year "Grand Tour" of Europe. As prosperous landlords, Samuel and Elizabeth entertained often. Their guests included Dr. Benjamin Rush, Benjamin Franklin, the Marquis de Lafayette, and George and Martha Washington. Franklin's daughter Sally wrote of dancing with George Washington at the Powels'. John Adams also referred to the Powel House after having dinner there, noting, "A most sinful feast again! Everything which could delight the eye or allure the taste." During one dinner attended by Washington, more than 160 dishes were served.

Samuel Powel died of yellow fever in 1793 after refusing to abandon the city and his duties as a Pennsylvania state senator. Elizabeth Powel stayed in the house and remained close friends with the Washingtons. Tradition holds that Elizabeth convinced Washington to accept a second term as president since she felt that only Washington's stature and integrity could keep the fledgling nation together.

By the early 1900s, the house had passed into other hands and uses. The new owners sold the home's remarkable interior wood and plasterwork to museums in Philadelphia and New York. In 1931, the Philadelphia Society for the Preservation of Landmarks—founded by

Powel House: Mayor Samuel Powel used the front room on the first floor for business. The elegant rooms on the second floor were used for formal entertaining.

Miss Frances Wister—saved the house and restored it to its late 18th century appearance. The home of "the Patriot Mayor" is open to the public and is one of the country's finest examples of a Georgian colonial townhouse.

244 South 3rd Street, Philadelphia, PA 19106 • (215) 627-0364

Built in 1786 by wealthy merchant Henry Hill, the Physick House on 4th Street is the only freestanding Federal-style home remaining in Society Hill. The neighborhood was named for the Free Society of Traders, a group of artisans, builders, and craftsmen who received large plots of land from William Penn in the 17th century. After the Revolution, wealthier residents began to move in, attracting such citizens as merchant William Bingham, who built a palatial residence in the area; Edward Shippen, whose daughter Peggy married Benedict Arnold; and Henry Hill, who made his fortune importing the popular Madeira wine.

Physick House: This home of Dr. Philip Physick was conveniently located just a few blocks from Pennsylvania Hospital.

Hill constructed an opulent 32-room house with a ballroom, several large bedrooms, and mirrored fireplaces made with Pennsylvania blue marble. In 1798, Hill succumbed to yellow fever, and Abigail Physick purchased the home. She deeded it to her brother, famous doctor Philip Syng Physick, who moved there in 1815. Physick had been one of the few doctors who stayed in the city to treat the victims of the 1793 yellow fever epidemic. Known as the "father of American surgery," Physick worked at the nation's first hospital, Pennsylvania Hospital, and pioneered many surgical instruments and techniques, such as the use of a stomach pump and cataract surgery.

After Physick's death in 1837, his family inhabited the home for several generations, but the house was later abandoned. In the late 1960s, publisher Walter Annenberg restored the Physick House and donated it to the Philadelphia Society for the Preservation of Landmarks. The house was designated a National Historic Landmark in 1976. It is open to the public as a museum.

★ ★ **PHILADELPHIA FIRSTS** ★ ★

Dr. Philip Physick created the nation's first soda pop in 1807, using the method pioneered by Schweppes in England. His soda was prescribed for gastric patients; he later added fruit syrup to improve the taste.

321 South 4th Street, Philadelphia, PA 19106 • (215) 925-7866

Thaddeus Kosciuszko was a Polish hero who fought for American independence and his own country's freedom. Born in 1746, Kosciuszko studied military engineering in Paris. Shortly after the adoption of the Declaration of Independence, he arrived in America and volunteered to join the American effort.

> *"General Kosciuszko is as pure a son of liberty as I have ever known...."*
>
> — Thomas Jefferson

One of Kosciuszko's first duties was fortifying the Delaware River against the British fleet's expected attack on Philadelphia. He also helped fortify Saratoga, where his engineering design contributed to the surrender of 6,000 British troops. This American victory convinced the French to support the American cause. Kosciuszko then became chief engineer at West Point, on the Hudson River. His fortifications prevented the British from bringing troops south from Canada using the river. At the end of the war, he was promoted to brigadier general.

Kosciuszko left for Poland in 1784 and led the 1794 Warsaw Uprising against the occupying Russians. He was badly wounded and imprisoned in St. Petersburg. Exiled from Poland, Kosciuszko returned to Philadelphia to consult Dr. Benjamin Rush about his wounds and to collect back pay. On August 18, 1797, Philadelphians lined the streets to welcome him. Kosciuszko convalesced at Mrs. Ann Relf's boardinghouse, receiving visitors such as Thomas Jefferson, Chief Little Turtle, and many young ladies, whom he sketched. Kosciuszko left Philadelphia in 1798. He died in Switzerland in 1817.

Thaddeus Kosciuszko National Memorial: The second floor window on the far left was Polish and Revolutionary war hero Kosciuszko's room.

The Thaddeus Kosciuszko National Memorial commemorates his brief residence on 3rd and Pine. Exhibits in English and Polish tell of his life and accomplishments on the first floor. Upstairs, the room he used has been restored to its 1798 appearance. The house is open to the public as part of Independence National Historical Park.

301 Pine Street, Philadelphia, PA 19106 • (215) 597-9618

On the corner of 6th and Lombard streets stands Mother Bethel African Methodist Episcopal Church. The church was founded by Bishop Richard Allen on land he bought in 1791. This land is considered to be the oldest piece of real estate in America continuously owned by African Americans.

Mother Bethel grew out of St. George's Methodist Church in Philadelphia. In 1786, Allen began preaching the 5:00 a.m. service at St. George's. As attendance grew, so did the dissention between blacks and whites. When Allen's parishioners were segregated to the balcony of the church, they peacefully left the congregation.

Working with Absalom Jones, Allen began fundraising to build a new church for the displaced parishioners. He made many powerful connections. Several whites contributed money to the site, including George Washington; Dr. Benjamin Rush, a signer of the Declaration of Independence and the "father of American psychiatry"; and William White, a bishop of the Episcopal Church.

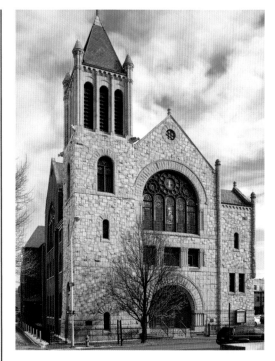

Mother Bethel Church: Today, the African Methodist Episcopal (AME) Church comprises 2.5 million members, 8,000 ministers, and 6,200 congregations.

In 1794, Allen established Mother Bethel, the first African Methodist Episcopal church. Mother Bethel's first building was an abandoned blacksmith's shed that was hauled by horses to the site. The church quickly grew, reaching nearly 500 members in 1805. In 1816, Allen met with 15 other representatives from African Methodist congregations to create a new denomination, the African Methodist Episcopal Church. It now numbers 2.5 million members.

Today, Mother Bethel Church is a National Historic Site. The present building, built in the 1890s, is the fourth to stand there. The church houses a museum with artifacts relating to the church and African American history and includes information about its role as a stop on the Underground Railroad.

419 South 6th Street, Philadelphia, PA 19147 • (215) 925-0616

Richard Allen, the founder of the African Methodist Episcopal Church, was born in 1760 into the slave-owning household of Benjamin Chew, a prominent Philadelphia attorney and judge. When Allen was seven, he and his family were sold to a Delaware farmer. Ten years later, his mother and three siblings were sold; he never saw them again. When Allen was 17, he heard the Gospel from a Methodist preacher and had a religious awakening. Allen persuaded his master to hear the preacher's sermon against slavery. After that, he was allowed to purchase his freedom for $2,000, which he earned in two years by doing extra jobs such as cutting cordwood.

Allen began preaching, and in 1786, he was invited to preach at St. George's Methodist Church in Philadelphia. The next year, he and Absalom Jones founded the Free African Society (FAS), a mutual aid society. Allen, Jones, and other members of the society worked heroically during Philadelphia's 1793 yellow fever epidemic, nursing the sick and burying the dead. More than 5,000 people died in three months, including some of their own members.

> "We considered it our duty to devise a plan in order to build a house of our own, to worship God under our own vine and fig tree."
>
> — Richard Allen, "The Doctrines and Disciplines of the African Methodist Episcopal Church," 1817

In 1792, Allen helped Jones to establish the African Episcopal Church of St. Thomas, the first independent black church in the country. Shortly thereafter, he founded Mother Bethel, an African Methodist Episcopal church. The congregation converted a blacksmith's shop to serve as its first church. In 1799, Allen was ordained as the country's first black Methodist minister.

In 1800, Allen married a former slave named Sarah—his second marriage. Together, they worked against slavery, helping many who had found refuge in their church, which was part of the Underground Railroad. He became the first bishop of the African Methodist Episcopal Church in 1816 and died in 1831. Allen's tomb includes the following inscription: "He was instrumental in the hands of the Lord in enlightening many thousands of his brethren, the descendants of Africa."

Drafting the Declaration: Thirty-three-year-old Thomas Jefferson wrote the Declaration of Independence in three weeks while lodging on the second floor of the Graff House.

On June 11, 1776, Thomas Jefferson and four other delegates were asked by the Second Continental Congress to write a declaration putting forth the reasons the colonies should sever ties with Great Britain. The committee's members—Benjamin Franklin, John Adams, Roger Sherman, and Robert Livingston—asked Jefferson to draw up the document.

Declaration (Graff) House: This 19th century rendering shows the Declaration (Graff) House. During that time, many historically important buildings were lost to change or decay.

Jefferson was renting two furnished rooms on the second floor of Jacob Graff's house on the edge of town at 7th and Market streets. He lived there with his enslaved servant Bob Hemings. The house was three and a half stories tall, with two rooms on each floor and a center stairway. Although by Jefferson's standards the house was small, it was surrounded by fields and removed from the nosier, busier areas near the waterfront.

Working from the Virginia Constitution as well as his extensive knowledge of political theory, Jefferson wrote the document in under three weeks. He submitted the document on June 28. The resolution for independence passed on July 2, 1776, and for the next two days, Congress debated and revised Jefferson's Declaration of Independence. It was adopted the morning of July 4, 1776.

Jefferson moved out of the home shortly thereafter, and the original structure was torn down in 1883. The National Park Service recreated the original building for the nation's bicentennial in 1976. Now known as the Declaration House, the building includes exhibits, a short movie, and a re-creation of the two rooms that Jefferson rented on the second floor.

Thomas Jefferson was a statesman, diplomat, scientist, architect, author, educator, lawyer, and plantation owner. Born in Virginia on April 13, 1743, he was the oldest son in a prominent slave-holding family. When Jefferson was 14, his father died, bequeathing him nearly 7,500 acres of land and 53 enslaved Africans.

Jefferson graduated from the College of William and Mary in Williamsburg and began practicing law. He also started building a massive estate he named Monticello—an architectural masterpiece that would occupy him for most of his life. In 1772, he married Martha Wayles Skelton, a widow.

> *"The wise know their weakness too well to assume infallibility; and he who knows most, knows best how little he knows."*
>
> —Thomas Jefferson, 1812

Jefferson began his political career in Virginia's House of Burgesses. He was elected to the Second Continental Congress in 1775, and he drafted the Declaration of Independence the following year at the age of 33. Soon after, he returned to Virginia to serve in the House of Delegates as a leader of the "progressive" party. He authored a bill to establish religious freedom in Virginia, an idea that later became part of the Bill of Rights, and served as governor of Virginia for two years. After the British invaded Virginia and almost captured him at Monticello, Jefferson retreated from public life. During that time, his wife died.

Presenting the Declaration: Thomas Jefferson (pictured holding the document) presents the Declaration of Independence to Congress in this image on the two dollar bill.

In 1783, Jefferson traveled to France, where he succeeded Franklin as minister. He took his daughter Patsy and sent for his daughter Molly, who was accompanied by her enslaved servant Sally Hemings. Returning to the United States in 1789, Jefferson became the first secretary of state under George Washington, and later became vice president under John Adams. In this role, he carried on bitter feuds with Alexander Hamilton, faced Federalist attacks, and cofounded the Democratic-Republican Party with James Madison. In 1800, he defeated Adams and became the third president of the United States. His election as president in 1800 drove the Federalists out of power.

Thomas Jefferson: As president, Jefferson doubled the size of the country with the Louisiana Purchase from France.

At the end of his second term as president, Jefferson retired to Monticello, where he worked to establish the University of Virginia. Jefferson died only a few hours before John Adams on July 4, 1826, 50 years after the adoption of the Declaration of Independence. Jefferson was 83.

Even before William Penn arrived in the New World in 1682, the Swedes had settled in Pennsylvania, constructing log homes and trading with the Native Americans. In 1646, Swedish settlers formed the Gloria Dei congregation. They met in a log church built in 1677. By 1700, however, they had moved to a new brick building.

Gloria Dei in South Philadelphia is the oldest church building in Pennsylvania and among the oldest in the country. Some notable people from the Revolutionary War are connected with Gloria Dei. Betsy Ross married her second husband, Joseph Ashburn, there in 1777. And Nils Collin, the Swedish pastor who served Gloria Dei from 1784 to 1831, was a close friend of Benjamin Franklin's. The remains of an early lightning rod (visible on the church's exterior) are reputedly a result of this friendship.

Gloria Dei became part of the Episcopal Church in 1845 after serving as the Swedish Lutheran Church for almost 150 years. In 1942, the church was designated a National Historic Site, six years before Independence Hall. The Gloria Dei congregation owns and maintains the building and the burial ground. The National Park Service maintains adjacent land to provide a buffer in case of fire in the built-up city.

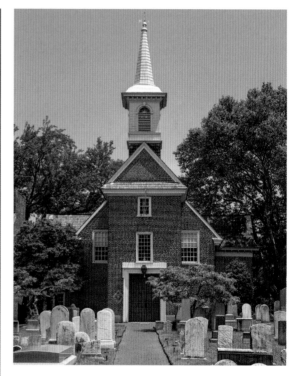

Gloria Dei Church: Because of his Quaker belief in religious freedom, William Penn allowed the Swedish Lutheran church to remain after he became proprietor of the colony.

The Germantown White House (Deshler–Morris House) is the nation's oldest surviving presidential residence. Located in Germantown, then a village about eight miles from the center of Philadelphia, the house was completed by merchant David Deshler in 1772. Five years later, it was at the center of fighting during the Battle of Germantown. British general William Howe occupied the residence for several months after the Americans retreated.

The Germantown White House: Washington stayed in the same house that had been inhabited by British General Lord Howe 16 years earlier.

In 1792, Colonel Isaac Franks purchased the elegant nine-room home from the Deshler family. He rented the house to President Washington in October 1793, when the deadly yellow fever epidemic raged through Philadelphia. There, Washington held cabinet meetings when he returned north from Mount Vernon. His cabinet consisted of only four men: Thomas Jefferson, secretary of state; Alexander Hamilton, secretary of the treasury; Edmund Randolph, attorney general; and Henry Knox, secretary of war.

Washington returned to the house with his family the following summer to enjoy the healthful countryside. This time, he brought his wife, Martha, and her two grandchildren: Nelly Custis and George Washington "Wash" Custis. The Washingtons had a large staff of paid, indentured, and enslaved servants. In Germantown, George and Martha entertained friends at dinner, attended the local church, and sent Wash to a local school. Washington enjoyed horseback rides with Nelly and went fishing with Wash.

The house was later sold to brothers Elliston and John Perot, and in 1834 it passed to Elliston's son-in-law, Samuel B. Morris. The Morris family lived in the house for over 100 years, carefully maintaining it because of its association with Washington. The family donated the home to the National Park Service in 1948. Now restored and furnished, it is part of Independence National Historical Park and located in the historic Germantown District.

5442 Germantown Ave., Philadelphia, PA 19144 • (215) 965-2305

Other Historic and Cultural Sites

After the Constitution of the United States was ratified, the government recognized the need to create a single national currency to replace the various state-issued bills and coins. In 1792, Congress met in Philadelphia to pass the Coinage Act, advocated by the secretary of the treasury, Alexander Hamilton. The new system replaced the English currency of pounds, shillings, and pence with dollars and cents. It also authorized the creation of a U.S. Mint in Philadelphia.

Early U.S. Coin: The Mint made trade much easier and safer, since all states used the same coins.

U.S. Mint: Coins minted in Philadelphia have a "P" on the face side of the coin.

The first Mint was located at 7th and Arch streets, just two blocks from the current Mint. The first coins minted at the facility were made from George Washington's household silver. Most citizens expected that the Mint would eventually move to the nation's new capital of Washington, D.C. Yet by the time the city was ready in 1800, the government lacked the money to construct a new Mint. In 1828, Congress passed an act that ensured the Mint would remain permanently in Philadelphia.

Four Mints have been built in Philadelphia since 1792. The Mint moved to its current building at 5th and Race streets in 1969, closer to its original location. While there are three other U.S. mints in operation in the United States today—Denver, San Francisco, and West Point—the Philadelphia facility is the largest in the world.

The Mint produces approximately 30 million coins worth about one million dollars each day. It also produces the Congressional Gold Medals and the Bronze Stars and Purple Hearts awarded to military heroes. Tours are available to the public.

151 North Independence Mall East, Philadelphia, PA 19106 • (215) 408-0112

In 1730, the worst fire in Philadelphia's early history burst from Fishbourn's Wharf on the Delaware River, burning all the stores on the wharf and three nearby homes. With Philadelphia's wood shingled

roofs, open hearth cooking, and candles, fires spread quickly. Concerned about the city's fire hazards, Benjamin Franklin wrote in the *Philadelphia Gazette* about the need for water pumping engines and firefighting equipment. The city council imported leather buckets, fire hooks, ladders, and engines from England, but still had no municipal fire department. In 1736, Franklin and members of his Junto club organized the Union Fire Company, the nation's first volunteer fire company. The Union Fire Company was so effective that several other volunteer fire companies were soon created. These organizations were a mainstay of the city until 1871, when the City of Philadelphia created its own municipal fire department.

Fireman's Hall: Volunteer fire brigades in the 18th century served an important role. At that time, most of the roofs in the city were made of wooden shingles and were highly flammable.

In 1752, Franklin started the nation's oldest fire insurance company, the Philadelphia Contributionship. This property insurance company is still in existence today and insures many historic properties, such as Carpenters' Hall. The Contributionship's symbol—four hands clasped together—can still be seen on the walls of many city buildings.

The Fireman's Hall Museum tells Philadelphia's rich history of firefighting. Located in the Old City, the museum is located in a restored 1902 firehouse. Artifacts in the museum include a hand water pumper used by Franklin, fire engines from the 1700s and 1800s, and fire marks from houses covered under Franklin's Contributionship. The free museum is run by the city's fire department.

149 N. Second, Philadelphia, PA 19106 • (215) 923-1438

For six years, Edgar Allan Poe lived in Philadelphia with his wife, Virginia, mother-in-law, Mrs. Clemm, and cat, Catterina. In the 1830s and 1840s, Philadelphia was the hub of the country's literary world, with many publishing houses and newspapers. Poe came to the city in 1838 and found work as a magazine editor to fund his writing. His first job was at *Burton's Gentleman's Magazine*, where he sold "The Fall of the House of Usher" for 10 dollars. Poe was a skilled editor. After George Graham bought *Burton's* magazine, he hired Poe. *Graham's* published Poe's "The Murders in the Rue Morgue" in 1841. This marked the beginning of a new genre—the detective story.

The Poe House: This three-story house was probably the nicest home Poe could ever afford. Then recently built, the brick house had a garden in the front where Poe's wife, Virginia, and her mother, Mrs. Clemm, often enjoyed the flowers.

During Poe's time in Philadelphia, he published more than 30 short stories, including "The Pit and the Pendulum," "The Black Cat," and "The Gold-Bug," for which he won 100 dollars. On April 6, 1844, the family left for New York, where Poe hoped to find a backer for his own literary magazine. He published the poem "The Raven," which brought him fame but little money. When his beloved wife died of tuberculosis two years later, his life began to spiral out of control. He fought poverty and despair and indulged in periodic binge drinking. He died in 1849.

The Edgar Allan Poe National Historic Site at 7th and Spring Garden streets is the only remaining Philadelphia house of several that Poe lived in. The house lacks Poe's furniture—when he moved to New York, he probably sold it—but there are exhibits and a short film about his life and literary contributions in an adjacent house. Tours of his house include the original cellar, which fits the description of the cellar in the story "The Black Cat."

Original Cellar in Poe House: Edgar A. Poe was a master at turning ordinary places into scenes of horror. In "The Black Cat," he described a basement that matches the one in his Philadelphia home, writing, "I had walled the monster up within the tomb!"

The Academy of Natural Sciences of Drexel University, founded in 1812, is the oldest natural history museum in the United States. During the early 19th century, the academy organized many expeditions to the West, following the 1804 to 1806 pioneering exploration of Meriwether Lewis and William Clark. On their expeditions, academy scientists gathered plant and animal species, which were catalogued and became the backbone of its 17-million specimen collection. Some of Lewis and Clark's specimens are also in the academy's collections.

The Academy of Natural Sciences: Founded in 1812, the academy explores the diversity of the natural world, focusing on a mandate of "useful learning."

The academy opened its doors to the public in 1828. It moved three times to keep up with its growth until it finally ended up at its current site on the Benjamin Franklin Parkway in 1876. Over the next 50 years, the academy's expeditions expanded beyond North America to include the Arctic, Central America, and later Asia and Africa. In 1948, the academy established an Environmental Research Division, one of the first in the country.

Now affiliated with Drexel University, the academy has an extensive collection of specimens, including a fossilized 45-foot-long, 7.5-ton, *Tyrannosaurus rex*, Lewis and Clark's plants, and Thomas Jefferson's fossil collection. There is a butterfly exhibit with live specimens and dioramas with mounted animals collected on expeditions. Other highlights include an exploration room, where academy staff members offer visitors the chance to touch various animals, and a collection of 30 different species of dinosaurs.

1900 Benjamin Franklin Parkway, Philadelphia, PA 19103 • (215) 299-1000

19th Century Entrance: The academy opened its doors to the public in 1828. Its current home on 19th Street and Benjamin Franklin Parkway was on the outskirts of town when it was constructed in 1876.

In 1824, Samuel Vaughan Merrick and William H. Keating established the Franklin Institute to honor Benjamin Franklin, advance his inventions, and promote interaction between inventors and scientists. The institute's first permanent home, built in 1825, is now the Philadelphia History Museum at the Atwater Kent (15 South 7th Street). But after more than 100 years, the institute had outgrown its space. In only 12 days, the institute raised more than five million dollars, despite the economic crisis, and the cornerstone of the new building was laid in 1932. The Fels Planetarium opened the following year, and the adjacent Franklin Institute Science Museum opened in 1934 as one of the first hands-on science museums in the country.

Over the years, the Franklin Institute has been the home of many "firsts" as scientists have showcased their technological innovations. In 1893, Nikola Tesla revealed principles of wireless telegraphy, and

★ ★ **PHILADELPHIA FIRSTS** ★ ★

The first courses in architecture taught in the United States were located at the Franklin Institute.

in 1934, Philo Taylor Farnsworth gave the world's first demonstration of an electric television system. The institute has also seen innovations in the weather bureau, in the standardization of machine parts, and in the promotion of the incandescent light bulb. The first architectural courses in America were also given here, under teachers such as Thomas U. Walter and William Strickland.

Today, the museum features interactive models of John Fitch's steamboat (1796) and Robert Fulton's steamboat, the *Clermont* (1807). It also has a steam engine that visitors can climb aboard, a fully equipped weather station, and exhibits on electricity.

Franklin Institute Science Museum: One popular exhibit in the science museum is a model of the human heart, which visitors can walk through.

One of the city's most iconic sites, the Philadelphia Museum of Art was established in 1876 as part of the country's Centennial Exhibition, held in Fairmount Park. The exhibition, which covered 285 acres, had pavilions from each of the states and exhibits from 37 foreign countries. It was host to more than 10 million visitors.

The Philadelphia Museum of Art: This Greek-style building crowns the end of Benjamin Franklin Parkway and features a bronze George Washington on his horse looking toward City Hall.

One of the exhibition's greatest legacies was its art gallery in Memorial Hall. One year after the exhibition closed, the gallery reopened as the Pennsylvania Museum and School of Industrial Art. In its early years, the exhibits consisted of industrial pieces as well as fine and decorative art such as books, antiques, jewelry, pottery, paintings, and textiles. The current building opened as the Philadelphia Museum of Art in 1928 and was designed by Julian Abele, the first African American to graduate from the University of Pennsylvania's architecture school.

★ ★ **PHILADELPHIA FIRSTS** ★ ★

The first World's Fair in the United States was held in Philadelphia in 1876, on the grounds of Fairmount Park, to celebrate the centennial anniversary of the Declaration of Independence.

The museum became legendary in pop culture in 1976 when the Oscar-winning movie *Rocky* captured a key scene on its 72 stone steps. Today, as one of the largest museums in the United States, the Philadelphia Museum of Art includes 80 period rooms and impressive holdings in Renaissance, American, Impressionist, and modern art.

2600 Benjamin Franklin Parkway, Philadelphia, PA 19130 • (215) 763-8100

Philadelphia Fountains: The refreshing fountains in the Center City District are a legacy from a 19th century effort to provide clean water for people and horses.

*I*n 1787, members of the Philadelphia Prison Society met in Benjamin Franklin's home. Their goal was to build a Quaker-inspired prison that would reform rather than just punish criminals—a contrast to the jails of the time, which were simply warehouses for prisoners. Forty-two years later, Eastern State Penitentiary was completed. The building was designed by the British-born architect John Haviland and consisted of seven cells surrounding a central surveillance rotunda. Each prisoner had his own cell with central heating, running water, a flush toilet, a skylight, and an adjacent private exercise yard. (By contrast, the White House had no running water and was heated with coal-burning stoves.)

Inside their cells, prisoners had only a Bible and a trade, such as shoemaking, to keep them busy. They were required to be hooded whenever they were outside their cells to prevent distraction, knowledge of the building, and interaction with guards. Proponents believed that silence would expose the criminals to the ugliness of their crimes, making them genuinely penitent.

Eastern State Penitentiary:
Like a medieval stone fortress, this prison was built to last. In fact, it was too expensive to tear down. Preservation and restoration efforts began in the 1990s.

Eastern State Penitentiary became the model for 19th century prisons. But debate grew about the effectiveness and compassion of solitary confinement. Eventually, the critics prevailed, and the Pennsylvania system was abandoned in 1913. The

★ ★ **PHILADELPHIA FIRSTS** ★ ★

The prison reform movement began in 1787 with the formation of the Philadelphia Society for Alleviating the Miseries of Public Prisons.

last prisoners left Eastern State Penitentiary in 1971, and the building stood empty until a tour program began in 1994. The Eastern State Penitentiary Historic Site now runs the former prison, giving tours and audio guides with commentary by both former guards and inmates. The prison is still in a state of semi-ruin.

2027 Fairmount Avenue, Philadelphia, PA 19130 • (215) 236-3300

On July 1, 1874, the Philadelphia Zoo opened its Victorian gates to the public, making it the first zoo established in the United States. Inspired by the zoos sprouting up in larger European cities, the Philadelphia Zoo featured nearly 700 birds, 131 mammals, and eight reptiles. More than 3,000 visitors came by foot, carriage, and steamboat to the zoo on its opening day, and within eight months, the zoo had received nearly a quarter of a million visitors.

★ ★ **PHILADELPHIA FIRSTS** ★ ★

The nation's first zoo, the Philadelphia Zoo, was opened to the public in 1874.

Many of the buildings on the zoo's 42 acres are historic. The most famous is the Solitude, built in 1784 by John Penn, grandson of William Penn. This elegant manor house is located along the banks of the Schuylkill River and is the only remaining house built by the Penn family. Other notable pieces of art and architecture include *The Dying Lioness* statue, which came from the Centennial Exposition in 1876.

The Philadelphia Zoo was the site of the first animal research facility in the country, established in 1901, and was the first zoo to feature a scientifically based, nutritionally balanced diet for its animals. In animal care, it was the first to exhibit reptiles,

America's First Zoo: The Philadelphia Zoo supports research efforts to protect polar bears, which are threatened due to global warming.

seen at its opening in 1874; the first zoo to have an orangutan birth, in 1928; the first to exhibit white lions, in 1993; and the first to breed endangered giant river otters, in 2004. Today, it is one of the region's most visited sites and a noted conservation organization, with 1,300 animals inhabiting its 42 acres.

3400 West Girard Avenue, Philadelphia, PA 19104 • (215) 243-1100

Lion Around: Big cats have been an important part of the Philadelphia Zoo since it opened in 1874.

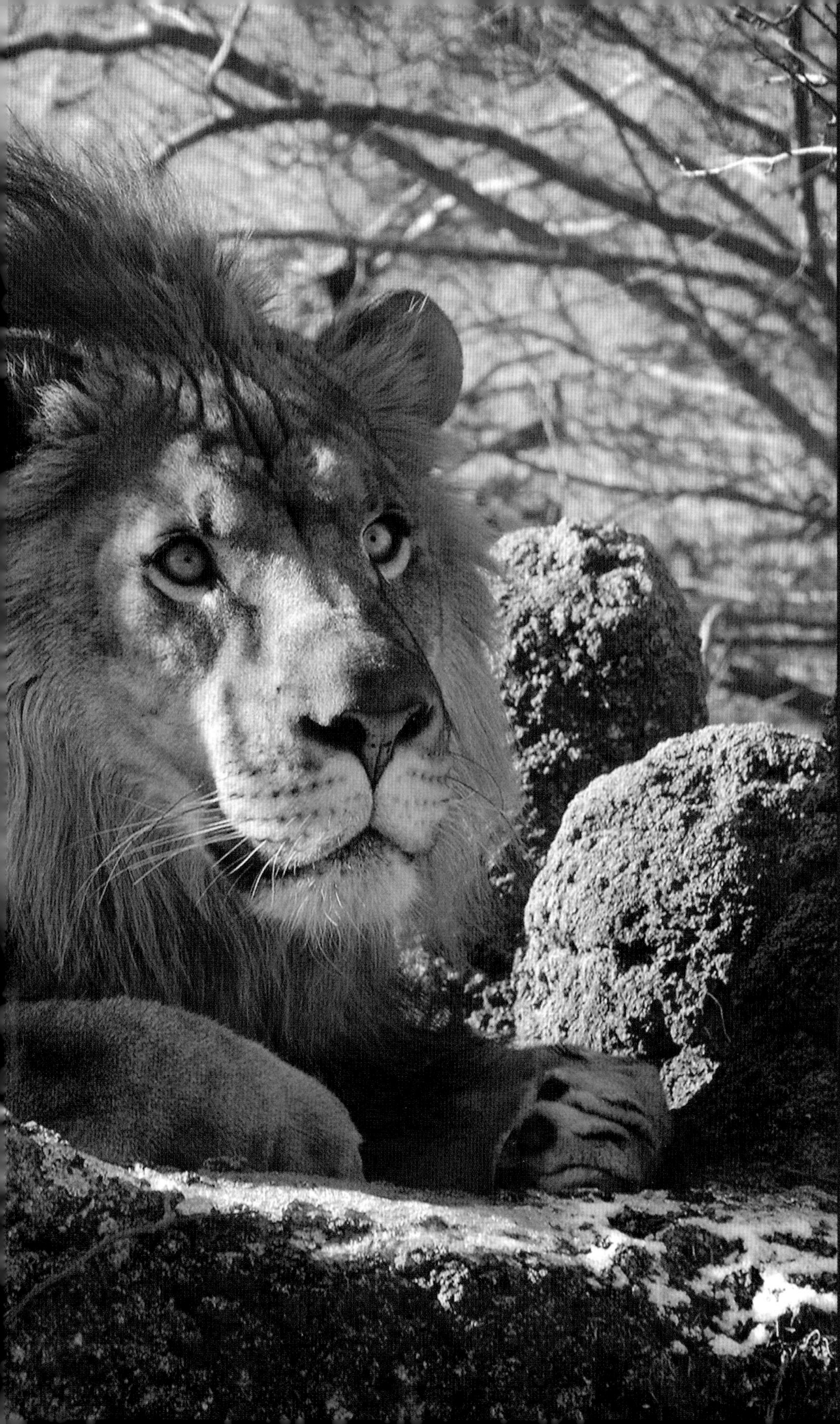

Philadelphia Zoo

The oldest continuously operating farmer's market in existence is the Reading Terminal Market, located in the heart of Philadelphia near City Hall. Markets have long been part of Philadelphia's history. In the 18th century, farmers, fishmongers, and butchers brought their wares to Philadelphia on Wednesdays and Saturdays and set up in wooden outdoor stalls. The largest market stretched from 2nd to 6th streets on High Street (now called Market Street). By 1859, however, the city shut down the outdoor stalls, citing traffic problems and health concerns.

Reading Railroad Terminal, circa 1900: The trains now run underneath the building, but fresh food still arrives daily.

The Reading Terminal Market opened in 1892. Built by the Reading Railroad as part of its downtown passenger terminal, the facility had space for hundreds of vendors in six-foot stalls and refrigerated space that could hold 200,000 pounds of meat and 50,000 crates of eggs. The market thrived for 60 years, but it struggled following the railroad's bankruptcy in 1971. In the 1980s, the railroad's Reading Company instituted a dramatic turnaround. Today, in this farmer's market, dozens of stands sell nearly every type of food, from Asian dishes to authentic Philly cheesesteaks. Vendors include Amish farmers selling shoo fly pie, an original 19th century tenant still scooping ice cream, restaurants serving full meals, and others selling flowers, crafts, jewelry, and clothing. More than 100,000 people pass through Reading Market each week, continuing a tradition that is more than a century old.

51 North 12th Street, Philadelphia, PA 19107 • (215) 922-2317

Reading Terminal Market: For more than 100 years, the Reading Terminal Market has sold a variety of produce, meats, and spices.

Interior Grand Staircase: This museum's Victorian building houses important works from many modern and contemporary American artists.

The Pennsylvania Academy of the Fine Arts is the oldest art museum and school in the nation, founded in 1805 by painter and artist Charles Willson Peale, sculptor William Rush, and other artists and business leaders. Peale was known through-out the nation for his portraits of Revolutionary heroes and had established a natural history museum in the State House for many years; Rush was considered the first major American sculptor.

> ★ ★ **PHILADELPHIA FIRSTS** ★ ★
>
> *William Rush, who cofounded the Pennsylvania Academy of the Fine Arts, was the first major American sculptor.*

The building opened in 1806, and the first exhibition debuted the following year. Classes began at the site in 1810, and in the early 1820s, a library and statue gallery were added. In 1844, the academy launched one of the nation's first formal training programs for women, designating particular days and places in which women could study art at the academy. It also used controversial methods of instruction, teaching both men and women to paint and sculpt from live nudes. In addition, its well-known anatomy program had students dissecting cadavers and animals to give them a better understanding of life forms.

Today, the Pennsylvania Academy of the Fine Arts houses an internationally renowned collection of 19th and 20th century American art by noted artists such as John Singer Sargent, Gilbert Stuart, Thomas Eakins, and Violet Oakley; contemporary artists including Bo Bartlett, Alex Katz, Faith Ringgold, and Robert Ryman; and prominent faculty and alumni. The current building—designed in 1876 by Frank Furness and George W. Hewitt—is considered one of the country's finest examples of Victorian Gothic architecture. The site was designated a National Historic Landmark in 1975 and was restored the following year.

Pennsylvania Academy of the Fine Arts: The museum's current building opened in 1876 and was restored in 1976. It is a National Historic Landmark.

118 North Broad Street Philadelphia, PA 19102 • (215) 972-7600

Betsy Ross House
www.historicphiladelphia.org/betsy-ross-house/what-to-see

Bishop White House and Todd House
www.nps.gov/inde/bishop-white-house.htm
www.nps.gov/inde/todd-house.htm

Carpenters' Hall
www.ushistory.org/carpentershall/index.htm

Christ Church and Burial Ground
www.christchurchphila.org/Historic-Christ-Church/Burial-Ground/59/

City Tavern
www.citytavern.com

Congress Hall
www.nps.gov/inde/congress-hall.htm

Declaration (Graff) House
www.nps.gov/inde/declaration-house.htm

Eastern State Penitentiary
www.easternstate.org

Edgar Allan Poe National Historic Site
www.nps.gov/edal/index.htm

Elfreth's Alley
www.elfrethsalley.org

Fireman's Hall Museum
www.firemanshall.org

Franklin Court
www.nps.gov/inde/franklin-court.htm

Free Quaker Meeting House
www.nps.gov/inde/free-quaker.htm

Germantown White House
www.nps.gov/demo/index.htm

Gloria Dei (Old Swedes') Episcopal Church
www.nps.gov/glde/index.htm

Independence Hall
www.nps.gov/inde/independence-hall-1.htm

Liberty Bell Center
www.nps.gov/inde/liberty-bell-center.htm

Library Hall
www.amphilsoc.org/about/campus/libraryhall

Merchants' Exchange Building
www.nps.gov/inde/merchants-exchange.htm

Mother Bethel Church
www.motherbethel.org/church.php

Old City Hall
www.nps.gov/inde/old-city-hall.htm

Pennsylvania Academy of the Fine Arts
www.pafa.org

Philadelphia Museum of Art
www.philamuseum.org

Philadelphia Zoo
www.philadelphiazoo.org

Philosophical Hall
www.apsmuseum.org

Physick House
www.philalandmarks.org/phys.aspx

Powel House
www.philalandmarks.org/powel.aspx

Reading Terminal Market
www.readingterminalmarket.org

Second Bank of the United States
www.nps.gov/inde/second-bank.htm

Thaddeus Kosciuszko National Memorial
www.nps.gov/thko/index.htm

The Academy of Natural Sciences of Drexel University
www.ansp.org

The Franklin Institute
www2.fi.edu

The President's House Site
http://www.nps.gov/inde/historyculture/the-presidents-house.htm

U.S. Mint
www.usmint.gov/mint_tours/?action=philadelphia

© *J. Alexander Baker III*; 25b; *Art Resource, NY*: 58-59; *Joshua Cogan/www.joshuacogan. com*: 10b, 15, 146a, 148, back cover a; © *Tom Crane*: 20a, 85, 92–93, 136, 153; *Stephen Durrenberger, pipevinestudio.imagekind.com*: 95; *Robert English*: 147; *Getty Images*: 1, 4–5, 7, 8–9, 11, 12, 13b, 14, 16, 17, 21a, 22, 24b, 27, 29a, 82–83, 90, 100, 106, 107, 108a, 110, 113a, 114, 121b, 125, 130–131, 142, 152, 154–155, 161, 162; *Peter Harholdt*: 102a; *Historical Society of Pennsylvania*: 36b; *Courtesy, Independence National Historical Park*: 21b, 33, 57b, 81b, 96-97, 98, 111, 116–117, 119a, 122b, 124, 126, 135b, 143; *Andrew Lewis. Available at www.flickr.com/rosemarybeetle*: 149; *Courtesy of the Library of Congress*: lc-usz62-49456: 34b; lc-uszc4-12141: 40; lc-usz62-17704: 41; lc-uszc4-1582: 45a; lc-dig-ppmsca-19468: 45b; lc-uszc4-2135: 48b ; lc-uszc4-4970: 50; lc-dig-pga-02794: 51a; lc-uszc4-2542: 51b; lc-dig-pga-02322: 53; lc-dig-pga-00249: 54-55; lc-dig-ppmsca-15715: 60; habs pa,51-germ,64–88 (ct): 61; lc-usz62-45561: 62a; habs pa,51-phila,111e—16: 62b; lc-dig-ds-02099: 63; lc-dig-pga-00927: 65; lc-uszc4-5280: 68; lc-dig-ppmsca-31505: 69, back cover c; lc-usz62-50375: 71a; lc-dig-ppmsca-24336: 72; lc-usz62-106865: 73a, lc-dig-pga-03236: 73b; lc-dig-pga-03855: 76-77; lc-usz62-73908: 78a; lc-uszc4-8071: 78b; lc-usz62-55021: 80; lc-dig-pga-01368: 84; lc-dig-pga-01669: 88; lc-dig-pga-03091: 91a, lc-dig-pga-01013: 91b; lc-uszc4-7214: 101; lc-dig-pga-01591 :103; habs pa,9-anda,1—34: 108b; lc-usz62-68175: 112; lc-usz62-123051: 115; lc-usz62-26670: 119b; lc-usz62-13002: 121a; lc-uszc4-5315: 123; lc-dig-highsm-12314: 127; lc-uszc4-9905: 128; habs pa,51-phila,25—3: 133; lc-usz62-2438: 135a; lc-usz62-128740: 138; lc-dig-pga-01533: 160; *Library of Congress, Prints & Photographs Division, Detroit Publishing Company Collection*: lc-d41-8: 10a; no. M 28060: 66-67; lc-dig-det-4a3128: 109; *Library of Congress, Prints & Photographs Division, Red Wing Adv. Co., Red Wing, Minn.*: Lc-uszc4-4971: 46–47; *Library of Congress, Prints & Photographs Division, Theodor Horydczak Collection*: lc-h8- c01-104-a: 141; *Photographs in the Carol M. Highsmith archive, Library of Congress, Prints and Photographs Division*: 75; *Library of Congress, Rare Book and Special Collections Division*: 34a, 57a; *American Philosophical Society (APS) Museum. Photo by Frank Margeson*: 99; *Pennsylvania Academy of the Fine Arts, Philadelphia*: 163; *Philadelphia Convention Visitors Bureau*: 2, 24a, 25a, 26b, 29b, 81a, 89, 102b, 104–105, 133, 144–145, 150, 151, back cover b; *Photo by Philadelphia Zoo*: 28, 157; *Photo by Philadelphia Zoo/Lisa Mann Gemmill*: 158–159; *Photo courtesy of Phillyhistory.org, a project of the Philadelphia Department of Records*: 36a; *Public domain*: 42, 48a, 71b, 113b, 122a, 134, 137, 139, 146b; *Janet A. Wilson*: 23b, back cover d; © *2006 Nicholas P. Santoleri, www.artist1.com*: 32; *Shutterstock*: 13a, 20b, 23a, 26a, 79, 140, 156, 168; *Concepts by Staib, ltd.*: 118; *age fotostock/SuperStock*: front cover; © *SuperStock*: 30-31; *Benjamin West, Penn's Treaty with the Indians, 1771–72*: 38-39, back cover d; © *George Widman*: 86–87